RFD ⁰/₁₄

Please return this book on or before the date shown above. To
renew go to www.essex.gov.uk/libraries, ring 0845 603 7628 or
go to any Essex library.

D1327033

The Finishing Touch

The Finishing Touch

Cosmetics through
the Ages

Julian Walker

The British Library

To Richard, Matthew and Mary

Thanks to Chantry Westwell, and the issue desk
staff of the Rare Books and Music Reading Room
at the British Library.

First published in 2014 by
The British Library
96 Euston Road
London NW1 2DB

Cataloguing in publication data
A catalogue record for this book is available
from the British Library

ISBN 978 0 7123 5752 4

Designed and typeset by
Briony Hartley, Goldust Design
Printed in Malta by
Gutenberg Press

CONTENTS

*The study of the beautiful, the desire to attain the ideal
of human perfection, the restless yearning implanted
in our innermost selves for all that is best and noblest,
materialised in the love of the beautiful, has played a part
in the world's history second only in importance to religion
and war.*
The Secrets of Beauty, Cora Brown Potter, 1914

INTRODUCTION

'The quest for physical beauty is essentially as old as Woman herself,' wrote Sonya Jolsen in *The Way to Beauty; a complete guide to personal loveliness*, in 1937. Certainly the desire to retain the beauty of youth has been a major impetus for us to exploit the world's natural, and unnatural, resources.

This book explores some of the materials and methods that have been used to help women – and men – enhance or hold on to their looks. It opens up a history of ingenuity, imagination and hope, but also of delusion, exploitation and self-harm.

Cosmetics has a complex and in many ways uncomfortable history. The question of whether cosmetics should be worn at all has taken many turns, from the disputes provoked by recent and current feminism to the moral debates of the early modern period. The anonymous writer of *A Discourse of auxiliary Beauty, or, artificiall Hansomenesse: in point of conscience between two ladies* (1692) was against all face-painting '... being a most ungodly practice, though generally (as they say) now used in England by Persons of Quality, who not content with Nature's stock of Beauty, do (not by a fine, but filthy art) add something to the advantage, as they think, of their complexions; but, as I fear, to the deforming of their Souls, and defiling of their Consciences'.

Puritan writers in the seventeenth century became very heated about several aspects of how wealthy women presented themselves, particularly over the matter of how much of the chest should be exposed, as seen in a number of portraits of aristocratic women. There was a lot of advice for women at this time regarding management of shape and weight; medical literature in the nineteenth century tended to see the female anatomy as primarily functional, and thus to be left to the dictates of nature.

But there has been a consistent view that there exists an ideal of female beauty – Agrippa von Nettesheim set about defining it in 1652: 'her flesh [should be] most soft and tender, her colour bright and lustring, Skinne cleare, Head comely, Locks faire, haire soft, shining, and long, her Countenance majesticke, Aspect pleasant, her Face surpassing in beauty, necke milke white, fore-head high, eyes sparkling with a lovely chearfulnesse ...' and so on. And therefore the author of *Beauties Treasury* (1705) pointed out that 'since the outside, by being most seen, does soonest captivate or repel the adorers' hearts, it must be allowed an innocent at least, if not necessary, care in the fair sex to cultivate beauty'.

The writer of *A Discourse of auxiliary Beauty* (1692) proposed that make-up was no more immoral than washing or taking medicine – all of these enhanced God's creation, the human form. To apply cosmetics was surely no worse than 'to wash that scurf and filth off which riseth naturally from our bodies by sweating or evaporation; or than the polling of men's hairs, and trimming of their beards, or paring their nails'. The argument cleverly pointed out cosmetic activity in men, the usual accusers.

It is questionable whether any of these arguments swayed anyone. A slyly flattering voice in *The Accomplished Ladies Rich Closet of Rarities* (1687) addresses its readers in a tone which understands the root of the desirability of make-up:

Gentlewomen, imagine not that I undertake this treatise to correct in you the least self-conceit or extravagant opinion of your merits, by putting into your hands an opportunity to render yourselves more beautiful, if possibly it may be; but to preserve what you have, at least from the ruins of time or any unfortunate accident—

The arguments continued through the eighteenth century, when it was proposed that white and red particularly distinguished a fashionable London complexion from a country one. For others, excessive make-up was put down to insidious French influence. 'Who would exchange the brilliancy of the diamond for the faint lustre of *French* paste? ... Let the *French* ladies white-wash and plaister their fronts, and lay on the colours with a trowel ...', wrote 'Rusticus' in *The Connoisseur* (12 December 1754); for France, as well as being the source of fashion, was seen as leading English beauties astray. A few weeks later *The Town* noted that a fashionable London artist refused to paint the portrait of 'a fine woman' because she wore too much make-up.

The arguments continue today – should we let natural beauty do the talking, or use products to enhance our qualities and hide our shortcomings? The cosmetics industry has clearly influenced this debate, but from the sixteenth to the eighteenth century women did not just wear make-up — they also took responsibility for making it, using their skills in distillation, filtering and judging when concoctions were ready for use. *The Ladies Dictionary* (1694) states that:

Every young Gentlewoman is to be furnished ... with very good stills, for the distillations of all kinds of waters, which stills must either be of tin, or sweet earth, and in them she shall distil all manner of waters ...

These stills would be used for medicine, cooking and cosmetics making. In many ways less wealthy women were better off; their lack of access to costly products protected them from harmful chemicals by restricting them to the use of herbal ingredients, or none at all. Though white lead face make-up may have been easier to apply than wheat starch or cyclamen root, and may have had the appeal of greater cost, its ill-effects were known from early on — so country girls found cheaper and safer alternatives. Pinching the cheeks produced red blushes; Hardy, in *Jude the Obscure* (1896), describes Arabella sucking in her cheeks to create dimples by an 'adroit little suck to the interior of each of her cheeks' — and it produced the desired results.

Ultimately, however, any artifice could only imitate the effects bestowed for all too short a time by Nature:

'Tis beauty truly blent, whose red and white
Nature's own sweet and cunning hand laid on ...
Twelfth Night, William Shakespeare, 1602

Underlying the whole business of cosmetics is a web of social structures and pressures, largely governed by the aspiration for women to achieve a proposed male ideal of female beauty. To approach a full understanding of this it is necessary to take into account several interdependent issues, such as competition between members of one sex for the attentions of the other sex, imagined ideals, and changing and manipulated fashions. Ultimately though, a large part of cosmetics is about women looking at themselves through male eyes. For much of the period under discussion here a woman's looks massively influenced her chances of securing a husband, and thus her status in society. The woman on the front cover applying 'the finishing touch' should excite our sympathy more than our ridicule; behind the lengths people went to in order to look young and attractive lie the spectres of fear and despair.

That said, many of the recipes presented here will provoke a wry smile, or a nod of recognition, as well as those which bring a shudder. I have not tried any of these recipes; if you should choose to do so, upon your own head (or face, neck, hands, etc.) be it.

COSMETIC WATERS
AND A LOVELY COMPLEXION

The word *cosmetic* means 'adorning' or 'beautifying'. Many of these recipes would do you little harm, but you might find some of the ingredients difficult to get hold of. The cost of some of them indicates the lengths people would go to to make reliable cosmetics: Hannah Woolley's 1672 recipe for 'a water to adorn the face' required the reader to distil melon roots, at a time when few people would have had access to such a luxury.

The desire for youthful looks could lead to the most outrageous claims being made for cosmetics; an early sixteenth-century manuscript states that 'The ladies and gentlewomen that will use often [this white face wash], were they seven score years of age, will show as they were but 3 years of age.' But the effect of a lifetime's use of cosmetics might ultimately have the opposite effect:

Lady Archer, having passed through all the stages, and disquietudes of fashionable life, has at length paid the debt of nature, the powers of medicine being found incompetent to resist the ravages of cosmetic art!
Bell's Weekly Messenger, 22 February 1801

To make the face look youthful

Take two ounces of aqua vitae, bean-flower water, and rose-water, each four ounces, water of water-lilies, six ounces; mix them all and add to them one dram of the water of tragacanth; set it in the sun six days, then strain it through a fine linen cloth; then wash your face with it in the morning, and do not wipe it off.
The Ladies Delight, Hannah Woolley, 1672

Tragacanth is a gum, of which only a small part dissolves in water, leaving the greater part as a soft mass. Water lily is used as a poultice to treat skin inflammations, so it makes sense that water-lily water would be good for the skin. Bean-flower water is, according to *A supplement to the pharmacopœias* (1828), by Samuel Frederick Gray, 'fragrant, cooling to the face and hands'.

A cosmetic water to enliven the spirits

Take one gallon of goats milk, and infuse into it the following ingredients, viz. four ounces of peach kernels, one pound and a half of wheaten bread, gourd seed, cucumber seed, lettuce seed, and melon seed, two ounces each; add to these the juice of four lemons, with the whites of twelve new laid eggs, and three ounces of sugar candy; distil the whole over a slow fire, and when it has stood to cool, let it be corked up in a bottle, and a few drops of it used from time to time.

N.B. This water should be kept by every lady, and as

it can be procured at a small expense, to neglect it is in a manner inexcusable.
The New London Toilet, 1778

Virgin's milk

This milk is obtained by pouring a great deal of water upon the dissolution of lead in vinegar. The liquor that results from this operation is as white as milk.

Another recipe:
Take what quantity of house-leek you please, beat it in a marble mortar, press out the juice, and clarify it. When you have a mind to use it, put a little of it into a glass and pour into the glass along with it some drops of the spirit of wine. In an instant will be formed a kind of curdled milk, very proper to make the skin smooth, and to take away red spots.
Abdeker: or, the Art of Preserving Beauty, 1756

This book was supposed to have been brought to Paris from the Middle East around 1740, and is a compilation of recipes built around the adventurous love story between a doctor and a young woman in a harem.

'Virgin's milk' was a longstanding term for a milky face wash, whose ingredients and composition varied. In the *Penny Cyclopædia* of 1835, virgin's milk was a solution of benzoin in alcohol, to which rosewater was added.

A water which makes women more beautiful

Take eight pounds of the feet and ears of hogs and calves, six pounds of rice water, two pounds of cows' milk, twelve fresh eggs, six ounces of crumbs of bread, a pound of fine sugar, and three pints of brandy. Mix all together; distil in a bath-heat [bain marie]; and add to the distilled liquor two ounces of roch-alum, an ounce of borax, two ounces of Benjamin, and a dram of milk. Digest all together in the sun for the space of twenty days; and before you use it wash your face with the decoction of vermicelli. This operation is to be repeated morning and evening, and it is one of the best methods that can be used for beautifying the skin.
Abdeker: or, the Art of Preserving Beauty, 1756

Given the rather large quantities involved, the mixture could not have lasted well. Hopefully it was not intended to be kept for the use of just one person. Roch-alum was alum in rock form.

Pigeon water

Take two white pigeons, pull them, and cast away the guts, head, wings and legs, then mince them into small pieces; then put them into a glass alembic, strewing the bottom with some plantain leaves; add thereto oil of sweet almonds three ounces, butter four ounces, a pint of goat's milk, the crumbs of a white loaf, borax and sugar candy, of each two drams, burnt alum and powdered camphor, of each three drams, the whites of 24 eggs; let all these

infuse for the space of twelve hours, then carefully stop the alembic, and distil them in balneo mariae; put the distilled water into glass phials to settle in a cool cellar; strain it through a fine cloth, and wash your face therewith mornings and evenings. It makes the face, or any other part, exceedingly comely; and it is that pigeon water which hath been so much apprised by the court dames at Paris.
Artificial Embellishments, Thomas Jeamson, 1665

Doves and pigeons, or sometimes just the fresh droppings of the birds, were a not infrequent ingredient in treatments for the skin.

A water to make the face bright

Take of the roots of lilies, cuckoo-pint, dragons, each half a pound; the water of bean-flowers a pint and a half; rose-water eight ounces. Distil them, adding musk and cinnamon, each two drams; and wash the face twice a day.
Cosmeticks, or the Beautifying Parts of Physick, Johann Wecker, 1660

Dragons was dragonwort, fortunately.

A water to beautify the face

Take of cuckoo-pint as much as is sufficient, bruise the thick parts with rose-water, dry them by the sun three or four days, and pouring more rose-water on it, use it.
The Ladies Delight, Hannah Woolley, 1672

The untreated tuber of cuckoo-pint (*Arum maculatum*) produces blisters when applied to the skin, but when heated and dried, this effect is neutralised. Distilling sometimes involved just collecting the drops of liquid that seeped out of a mixture.

A good complexion

English women are famed for their dazzlingly fair complexions; this comes from the extreme care their mothers take in seeing that their children always wear gauze veils, and that their diet principally consists of white meats with an abundant use of milk. I know that it is impossible to have a fine complexion if care is not taken to diet oneself properly, and to avoid anything that is harmful, such as salt meat or fish, curries, and all highly spiced dishes, shell fish, cheese, pastry, dark meats, beer and spirits of all kinds.
Beauty and How to Keep it, 'A Professional Beauty', 1889

Diet has alwys been seen as a contributing factor in keeping a beautiful body, though the thinking governing how this works, has seen many changes. 'A Professional Beauty' seems to have the idea that the colour of your food at least partially governs the colour of your skin.

Puppy-dog water

To make pig, or puppydog, water for the face
   *Take a fat pig, or a fat puppydog, of nine days old,
and kill it, order it as to roast, save the blood, and sling
away nothing but the guts; then take the blood, and pig,
or puppydog, and break the legs and head, with all the
liver and the rest of the innards, of either of them;
put all into the still if it will hold it; to that, take two
quarts of old canary [wine], a pound of unwashed
butter not salted, a quart of snail-shells and also two
lemons, only the outside pared away; distil all these
together in a rose-water still, either once or twice; let it
drop slowly into a glass bottle, in which let there be a
lump of loaf sugar and a little gold-leaf.*
**The Ladies Dressing-Room Unlock'd and her Toilette
Spread, Mary Evelyn, 1700**

It is not clear exactly how much of this is a satire on
the excesses of make-up in a period when women
wore coiffures which nearly doubled their height,
and dresses which could not fit through doorways —
the 'farming' of dogs shocks modern sensibilities but
would have been less shocking then. The text appears
in a book which contains a fairly gentle satirical
poem on women's costumes and make-up, and a 'fop's
dictionary'; so, all things considered, this is probably
not a straightforward recipe — 'puppy-dog water'
was usually the urine from a puppy, used in cosmetic

preparations. But the following recipe appears in a popular book on cosmetics and perfumes, which went through several editions:

A cosmetic water to nourish and conserve the delicacy of the complexion

Take four calves feet, bone them, put them to soak for nine days in water, which you must renew twice a day; then put them in a glass alembic; then add:

The whites of two dozen eggs, with the shells.

A pound of calves cheek, washed and degreased, cut into pieces.

A chicken skinned alive, of which you should remove the head, entrails and feet, and which you should also cut into pieces.

A sliced lemon.

Half an ounce of crushed white poppy seeds.

The inside of half a loaf of bread, crumbled.

Four little dogs, one or two days old.

Three buckets of goats milk.

Distill them in a bain-marie; this distillation will take a long time, but it must be continued and kept going until almost dry, that is to say, just to the point where it will produce nothing more.

This water is excellent to nourish the skin and conserve the delicacy of the complexion.

Traité des Odeurs, Antoine Harnot, 1777

To improve the Complexion

---

*Dissolve flowers of sulphur in milk, and strain clean.
When used, take care not to disturb any sediment of the
sulphur that may remain.*
The Englishwoman's Domestic Magazine, 1 October 1852

Sulphur soap is still a recommended way of dealing with
skin problems.

How to cure chaps in the face

---

*When the injurious violence of wind or weather hath rent
your silken skins, if you intend to unite the separating
parts, you will find these your serviceable cements:*

*Take stag's suet and goat's suet, of each half an ounce;
burnt borax, two drams; new wax, half an ounce; oil of
roses, two drams. Make it into an ointment and use it. Or
else take capon's grease and camphor, mix them and anoint
the chaps therewith every night; in the morning wash
with bran and water. Some dissolve mouth glue in warm
rosewater, and anoint the face therewith.*
Artificial Embellishments, Thomas Jeamson, 1665

'Chaps', the cracks from chapped skin, would presumably
appear on the lips; the word is related to 'chop', in the sense
of a cut. 'Mouth glue' is, or was, glue made from boiled
'hoof and hide'; the jelly would be moistened by mouth
before application, presumably as a barrier in this case.

Two ways to gain a good complexion

Take madder, frankincense, myrrh, oriental saffron, mastic, of each like quantities; bruise them all, and steep them in white wine; anoint the face therewith before going to bed; in the morning wash either with cold or warm water; it will purple any part with a gallant and pleasing blush. Or take fraxinella roots, chew them, and tie them in a fine rag, and bathe the face.

This following is much commended for making the face white and clear as alabaster. Take myrrh two ounces, frankincense half an ounce, white ginger three drams, cinnamon and sublimate of each two drams, camphor one dram, whites of three or four eggs; put all these together in the belly of a young capon or pullet well washed and cleansed; add thereto goats' or asses' milk, distil all together, and you shall have such a water that few things can equal it.

***Artificial Embellishments,** Thomas Jeamson, 1665*

Note the instruction to activate one of the ingredients by chewing it.

A secret for preserving the skin of the face

When you go to bed at night, apply to your face some slices of veal. There is no topic so efficacious as this for taking away wrinkles, for keeping the skin supple, and preserving a fresh complexion.

***Abdeker: or, the Art of Preserving Beauty,** 1756*

An excellent receipt to clear a tanned complexion

At night going to rest bathe the face with the juice of strawberries, and let it lie on the part all night, and in the morning wash yourself with chervil water. The skin will soon become fair and smooth.
The Toilet of Flora, 1775

A fake anti-tan?

A Simple Home Remedy for Tanning

Scrape a teaspoonful of horseradish into a cup of sour milk; let it stand six hours before using.
The Woman Beautiful, Ella Adelia Fletcher, 1899

This is to get rid of a tan.

An oil to colour the face

Take of common oil, rosemary flowers, each one part; mix them and put them in a glass vial under horse dung, for three weeks or a month, then strain it and set it in the sun for some days, and so use it.
Cosmeticks, or the Beautifying Parts of Physick, Johann Wecker, 1660

The horse dung would have kept the mixture at a constant

warm temperature; setting it in the sun would probably have broken down some of the colour.

Five Waters

Lavender water

Take fresh or dried lavender flowers, sprinkle them with white wine, brandy, molasses spirit or rose-water, and let them stand in infusion for some days, and then distil off the spirit. The distilled water will be more odoriferous if the flowers are dried in the sun in a glass bottle close stopped, and white wine afterwards poured thereon.

If you would have speedily without the trouble of distillation a water impregnated with the flavour of lavender, put two or three drops of oil of spike [lavender], and a lump of sugar into a pint of clear water or spirit of wine, and shake them well together in a glass phial with a narrow neck. This water, though not distilled, is very fragrant.

To make rose-water

To make an excellent rose-water let the flowers be gathered two or three hours after sun-rising in very fine weather, beat them in a marble mortar into a paste, leave them in the mortar soaking in their juice for five or six hours, then put the mass into a coarse canvas bag and press out the juice; to every quart of juice add a pound of fresh damask roses, and let them stand in infusion for twenty-four hours; then put the whole into a glass alembic, and place it in a sand heat [hot sand]. Distil at first with a gentle fire, which is to be increased gradually till the drops follow each other as quick as possible; draw off the water as long as it continues to run clear, then put out the fire, and let the alembic stand until cold. The distilled water at first will have very little fragrancy, but after being exposed to the heat of the sun about eight days, in a bottle lightly stopped with a bit of paper, it soon acquires an admirable scent.

Sweet honey-water

Take of good French brandy a gallon, of the best virgin honey and coriander seed, each a pound, cloves an ounce and a half, nutmegs an ounce, gum Benjamin and storax, of each an ounce, vanillas four, the yellow rind of three large lemons; bruise the spices and benjamin, cut the vanillas into small pieces, put all into a cucurbit [type of glass vessel] and pour the brandy on them; and after they have digested forty-eight hours, distil off the spirit in a retort with a gentle heat.

To a gallon of this water add of damask rose-water and orange-flower water, of each a pint and a half, musk and ambergris, of each five grains; first grind the musk and ambergris with some of the water, and afterwards put all together into a large matrass [type of glass vessel], shake them well together, and let them circulate three days and nights in a gentle heat, then let all cool; filter and keep the water in a bottle well stopped for use.

It is an antiparalytic, smoothes the skin, and gives one of the most agreeable scents imaginable. Forty or sixty drops put in to a pint of clear water are sufficient to wash the hands and face with.

Venice Water, highly esteemed

In the month of May, take two quarts of a black cow's milk, pout it into a bottle with eight lemons and four oranges, sliced; add an ounce of sugar-candy, and half an ounce of borax, distil in a water bath or sand heat.

This water is counterfeited at Baghdad in Persia, in the following manner. Take twelve lemons peeled and sliced, twelve new laid eggs, six sheep's trotters, four ounces of sugar candy, a large slice of melon, and another of pompion [pumpkin], and two drachms of borax; distil in a large glass alembic with a leaden head.

A cosmetic water

Wash the face with the tears that issue from the vine, during the months of May and June.
The Toilet of Flora, 1775

Venice Water sounds rather exciting with its very specific ingredients and instructions, and the mysterious counterfeiting.

Face packs

Mud or clay packs suit the greasy skin. In this country the best and most popular form of mud is fuller's earth, which comes from Reigate. Radioactive packs are made from mud taken from the river St Gellert. Special qualities are also claimed for mud packs made from clay from La Toja in north-west Spain.

To prepare a mud or clay pack for a greasy skin with large pores, make some fuller's earth into a smooth paste with equal parts of witch-hazel and rosewater, to which a few drops of eau de Cologne have been added. Mix the liquids together before moistening the mud. A pack with stronger astringent properties can have camphor water as a substitute for the rosewater, or a larger quantity of eau de Cologne and a few drops of benzoin, but experiment with the milder pack first. A variation of this pack for the same type of skin is made by mixing the mud with equal parts of 10 vol. peroxide and witch-hazel. This pack would serve as a bleach as well as an astringent treatment.
The Way to Beauty; a complete guide to personal loveliness,
Sonya Jolsen, 1937

A radioactive face pack: perhaps rather too astringent.

THE FACE, CHIEF
SEAT OF BEAUTY

Whether or not the writer of *Abdeker* was right in claiming that the face is the chief seat of beauty, there can be little doubt that it is the chief site of cosmetics.

The face is the chief seat of beauty; it there displays all its force and all its majesty; it is there it places those powerful charms that command and captivate the spectator's heart, and excite his admiration.
Abdeker: or, the Art of Preserving Beauty, 1754

Agrippa von Nettesheim (*The Glory of Women*, 1652) was more specific in his description of the ideal female face: 'eye-browes smooth and thin, divided with decent distance, from the middle of which descendeth her nose, straight and of due proportion, under which is her mouth neat, round and lovely, with small, fresh, and red lips'.

To embellish the face

Take 12 lemons, cut them into little slices, as many new laid eggs with their shells, borax and white sugar candy 2 ounces, a melon, half a pompion [pumpkin], six calves feet, of vinewater one pound, spermacetti two ounces, flowers

The only Delicate

Beautyfying Cream,

For the

FACE, NECK, and HANDS.

LONDON, Printed in the Year 1716.

of white water lily cut 2 ounces, and mix all these dregs
very small, mix and distil them in a glass alembic, in Bain
Marie. This secret was given by a lady, a physician, who
had made a French lady pay £50 for it, and is excellent.
John Evelyn's papers, 1650s

'Spermacetti' (spermaceti) is a waxy substance taken from
the heads of hunted sperm whales, traditionally much
used in cosmetics.

The ears

The ears are a great ornament to the head when they are
well shaped, do not exceed a certain size, are neatly placed,
well-bordered, and have all those little vermicular turnings
and windings (which compose the external parts of this
organ) in perfection.

Where the ear is right placed, it lies so close to the head,
that you cannot put a piece of the thinnest paper between
them, without moving the former. You cannot, therefore, be
at too much pains to make the ears of children lie neatly.
And here we must reflect on the very improper method
practised in some schools, of punishing children by pulling
their ears.
Hebe; or, the Art of Preserving Beauty, 1786

With the demise of school caps we have probably also lost
the charming custom of mothers tucking in their sons'
ears to encourage them to grow closer to the scalp.

Care of the ear

*The ear requires to be daily washed with soap and water,
and carefully dried; laving the back of the ears with
cold water contributes to preserve the teeth; internally it
is necessary to remove the cerumen when it becomes too
copious. The corner of a fine towel rolled up to a nice
point, and dipped in tepid soapy water, will sufficiently
cleanse the passage and remove the superfluous wax in
ordinary cases. Picking the ear is a most pernicious habit,
and has been ascertained to be the cause of several severe
affections.*
Toilet Table Talk, 1856

How to beautify the forehead

*The forehead is the ivory throne where Beauty sits in state;
it must therefore be smooth and raised to a decent height,
for if it be too low it is much beneath the grandeur of her
commanding majesty; and if furrowed with wrinkles it
will put her too much in mnd of human frailty to take a
pleasing recreation there.*

*To make the forehead high eradicate the hairs which
encroach too much upon its bounds thus: take as much
mastic as you shall have occasion to use, keep it in warm
water till it be so soft that you can spread it upon a fillet,
then bind that fillet [headband] to the forehead all night,
and in the morning twitch it off. So you may take hair from
any part of the body.*
Artificial Embellishments, Thomas Jeamson, 1665

An antecedent of wax strips. Many seventeenth-century recipes for dealing with excess hair are much less similar to current ones, for example:

Take the gall of an eel, mix it with oil of roses, or the blood of a bat, and use it. Or take quicklime, lizards' dung, boil them in an equal quantity of vinegar and oil of henbane till the vinegar be consumed; make it into an unguent for your use.
Artificial Embellishments, Thomas Jeamson, 1665

It seems improbable that oil of roses could be satisfactorily substituted by the blood of a bat. Quicklime applied to any part of the body would certainly remove more than unsightly hair.

An excellent oil to take away the heat and shining of the nose

Take twelve ounces of gourd-seed, crackle them, and take out the kernels, peel off the skins, and blanch six ounces of bitter almonds, and make an oil of them, and anoint the place grieved therewith; you must always take as much of the gourd-seed as of the almonds; use it often.
The Queen's Closet Opened, 1696

Gourd seeds yield an oil possibly good for wounds and burns; sweet almond oil is an emollient, but the oil from bitter almonds yields glucose, benzaldehyde and the toxic cyanide, carrying a strong almond smell.

A red nose

A red nose is, for a woman, a calamity. It is not only unbecoming in itself, but it has become associated with the idea of most degrading vices. Thus it is doubly ugly. The only remedies – or rather preventives, for they are better used as such – are careful attention to cleanliness, diet, exercise, and abstinence from tight lacing.
Talks on the Toilet, 1856

This is rather harsh in its assumption of the connection between a red nose and alcoholism, or worse. Why should not make-up and powder render a red nose as fair as any other feature? But there is much to be said for the recommendations.

Remedies for the defects of the nose

The nose is a very great ornament of the face, and Beauty is a very nice and cleanly dame, who loves to have the nose (though but the sink of the brain to convey from it what is noxious) kept neat and handsome as well as the other parts designed for more honourable uses. If there be then any obstruction, soreness or any other thing that appears unseemly, or occasions offence to the smelling of the nose, as being afflicted with some sore or ulceration:

Take calamus aromaticus, galingale, damask roses and lavender dried and powdered of each two drams, mix them well, and snuff a little up the nose at a time,

or

Take London Treacle two drams, dissolve it in two ounces, and snuff a little of it into your nostrils very warm, and do this often.

or

Often sponge or wash your nostrils with a little fine rag at the end of a stick, dipped in white wine, wherein rose-leaves have been concocted, and it will not only cure the distemper, but render your breath and smelling pleasant.
Beauties Treasury 1705

According to one recipe London Treacle was a mixture of oil, gunpowder and sherry.

A chin patch

Then Spanish Snush [snuff], to Modish Nose is put,
At which Perfumed Handkerchief's drawn out;
T'adjust some bold disorder in the Face,
And put the Chin-patch in its proper place.
Sylvia's Revenge, Richard Ames, 1688

A chin patch served the same purpose as a beauty patch, either drawing attention to the form of the chin, or covering an unsightly blemish. In this case it seems to have slipped, and its repositioning is hidden behind a handkerchief.

Dorothy Dimple

I, too, wonder why women get fat about the chin. Happily, I can tell you of something you have not tried, and that is the 'Kalopia', or muscle beautifier, a cleverly designed little instrument to be worn at night, to restore and preserve the contour of the face and neck. Madame Allenby (Face Specialist, etc.), 3, Saville Street, Hull, who has recently invented this, will send it to you, and a bottle of cream for use with it, post free for 30s 6d.

Health and Home, 20 September 1900

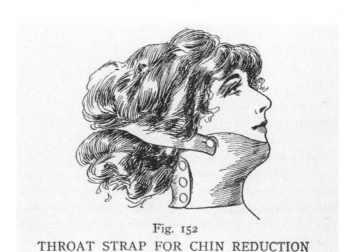

Fig. 152
THROAT STRAP FOR CHIN REDUCTION

To kill and take away worms in the nose, or any part of the face, that spot and blacken it with their blackheads peeping even in the skin

These worms in some are very numerous insomuch that their faces appear as if they were spotted over with sparkles of gun-powder, besides they cause an itching or pricking pain, as being generated of a salt lodging in the porous parts of the skin.

Take the juice of lemons two ounces, unslaked lime two drams, powder of sulphur one dram, let them infuse over a gentle fire till well incorporated, then dip a feather or a fine rag into it, and stipple the face, lips or nose where the worms lurk, and in often so doing it will kill them, then stipple the skin with warm water and oil of sweet almonds, and the pores being so opened, you may easily squeeze them out with your thumb and finger, then wash the place with juice of lemons alone, and not any more will appear there, especially for a very considerable time.
Beauties Treasury, 1705

The idea that blackheads were actually alive persisted into the nineteenth century, with Lola Montes, of whom more later, calling them 'flesh-worms' as well as 'black specks', though she added that only 'ignorant people suppose them to be little worms'.

Blackheads

The small black spots and marks frequently observed on the skin in hot weather, particularly on the face, generally arise from the accummulation of the indurated solid matter of the perspiration in its pores. When they assume the form of small pimples (acne punctata) and often when otherwise, they may be removed by strong pressure between the fingers, or between the nails of opposite fingers, followed by the use of hot soap-and-water. The subsequent daily application of a weak solution of bichloride of mercury, as in the form commonly known as Gowland's lotion, or of sulphate of zinc, will completely remove the swelling, and generally prevent their reformation.

The Toilet and Cosmetic Arts, Arnold Cooley, 1866

How often teenagers are told 'don't squeeze a spot' – and how often the temptation is too strong … Cooley's encouragement to attack both spots and blackheads with the nails would not find favour now, though Gowland's lotion could do worse to your skin. By this time various recipes were generically called Gowland's lotion – Mrs Beeton's *All About Everything* (1871) gave a recipe which included bichloride of mercury, with the proviso that it 'must be used with care, as it is a poison'.

How to take away any pimple from the face

*Brimstone [sulphur] ground with the oil of turpentine,
and applied unto any pimple one hour maketh the flesh to
rise spongeous; which being anointed with the thick oil of
butter which ariseth in the morning from new milk sodden
a little overnight, will heal and scale away in a few days,
leaving a fair skin behind. This is a good skinning salve.*
Delightes for Ladies to Adorn their Persons, 1636

Turpentine is a skin defatting agent and sensitiser, and
prolonged contact can cause dermatitis; best not tried.

A water to prevent freckles or blotches on the face

*Take wild cucumber roots and narcissus roots, of each an
equal quantity, dry them in the shade and reduce them to
a very fine powder, which put into strong French brandy,
and wash the face therewith till it begins to itch; then wash
with cold water. This must be repeated every day till a
perfect cure is obtained, which will soon happen, for this
water has a slight caustic property, and of course must
remove all spots on the skin.*
The Toilet of Flora, 1775

Black patches

Smallpox, one of the killer diseases of the early-modern period, left survivors with pockmarks on the face – 'pox' was originally 'pocks'. Beauty spots or patches, also called *mouches*, served to cover these, though it is debatable whether this was their first intended use – it is reasonably claimed that they made the skin look whiter by contrast. They might be red as well as black, and were made of silk, taffeta, velvet, paper or leather attached with gum, and were by no means limited to circular in shape: hearts, stars, moons, castles and animals were all popular. Naturally puritan commentators objected to them, seeing them as tokens of death and marks of shamelessness. Hannah Wolley, author of *The Gentlewoman's Companion* (1682), wrote:

I am afraid that the black oath of God-damn-me in the mouth of a Ranter, and the Black-patch in the face of a Gentlewoman, are near of a kin one to another.

And the writer of *England's Vanity* (1683) wrote:

Methinks the mourning coach and horses (all in black) and plying in their foreheads, stands ready harnessed to whirl them to Acheron, though I pity poor Charon for the darkness of the night.

During the reign of Queen Anne (1702–14) political affiliations were shown by the side of the face on which the patches were worn. *Abdeker*, the fanciful tale of a French man's love for a Turkish girl, proposed that the origin of patches lay in the story of a fly which landed near the heroine's eye while she was being made up – hence the name *mouche* ['fly' in French]. The contrast which it gave to the pale skin colour was recreated using a false patch. The book goes on to list the names for specific patches:

At the exterior of the eye – Killing
In the midst of the forehead – Majestic
That placed in the fold that is formed in the skin by laughing – Jovial
That in the midst of the cheek – Gallant, or Jiltish
That near the lips – Coquet, or Prude

SNOW WHITE AND ROSE RED

It was long supposed that the desire to emulate Queen Elizabeth I's light skin was the the inspiration for white face make-up. More likely it came from France, where a recipe for whitening the face can be found in the late thirteenth-century text *Li Romanz du Mont Saint-Michel*. But perhaps the increasing use of mirrors in the sixteenth century accelerated the process.

There were several ways of creating a white skin; some of them harmless, and others toxic and recognised as such. A manuscript from around 1510 in the Harley Collection offers a recipe for ceruse (white face paint) which is made 'not after the usual manner, so that women may obtain their purpose without loss of the skin or teeth'. While the extremely wealthy could afford to use ground pearls, cheaper alternatives such as rice starch clogged the pores and tended to fall off. Most alarming was a mixture containing bismuth oxynitrate (Spanish white), which turned black in contact with sulphurous fumes from coal fires.

A proven ointment to whiten

*Take the root of lovage and some root of the dwarf
elder or danewort and some common mallow; boil together
and wash. Next take fresh lard of pig and two egg-whites,
as much of the one as of the other, stir together very
well and apply. Next take some lovage and some mallow
and boil together. And wash with water in the morning
after application.*

Li Romanz du Mont Saint-Michel, late thirteenth century

A water to whiten the face

*Take of the juice of lemons one ounce, of Venus-shell five
ounces; steep them till they are dissolved, then add twelve
lemons sliced, ten whites of eggs, camphor and borax, of
each one dram and a half, water of pine-apples half a pint.
Mix and distil them.*

**Cosmeticks, or the Beautifying Parts of Physick, Johann
Wecker, 1660**

Lemon juice is surprisingly strong, and its acid content
would over time dissolve the material of a shell, which
is mainly calcium carbonate. This would have been an
expensive recipe, as pineapples were reputedly not grown
in England before 1675.

To make a blaunch for any Ladies face

Take of white Tarter two drams, Camphire one dramme, Coperas halfe a dramme, the whites of foure egges, juyce of two Lymonds, oyle of tarter foure ounces, Plantane water as much, white Mercuri a pennyworth, bitter almonds two ounces, all must be powdred and mixed with the oyle and water, and then boyled upon a gentle fire, and straine it and so keepe it: The partie must rub her face with a scarlet cloth, and then over night wash her with it, and in the morning wash it off with bran and white wine.

For a fayre face, proved another way

Take Plantane and white vineger, and still them together, and wash your face therewith fifteene dayes, morning and evening, and after this, drinke a draught of vineger in the morning once in three dayes.

To make the face white and faire

Take Rosemary and boyle it in white wine, and wash thy face therewith, and you shall be faire, then take Erigan, and stampe it, and take the juyce thereof, and put it all together, & wash thy face therwith, prob [proven].
A Closet for Ladies and Gentlewomen, 1608

These three recipes, all from the same source, provide a range of approaches to getting a white skin.

A water to make the face look white

Take of live sulphur one ounce, white frankincense two ounces, camphor one dram, rose-water a pint, powder them and mix them, and set them in the sun nineteen days, and wash the face with it at night. But in the morning wash it with the decoction of bran and roses.
Cosmeticks, or the Beautifying Parts of Physick, Johann Wecker, 1660

The morning wash seems to be a good facial scrub. 'Live sulphur' was naturally occurring, uncombined sulphur, a mineral which is used in the treatment of skin conditions such as psoriasis and eczema – with sulphur soap being a common material for treating dry skin.

To anoint the face and to make it white

Take fresh bacon grease, and the whites of eggs, and stamp them together, and a little powder of bays and anoint your face therewith, and it will make it white.
Delightes for Ladies to Adorn their Persons, 1636

Oil pressed from bayleaves has for a long time been used as a treatment for skin problems, so powdered dry leaves might have had some beneficial effect, but probably not enough to counter the unpleasantness of lard after a few hours.

White face make-up

White face make-up, known as ceruse, was applied as a white powder rubbed on to the skin. The most famous formula, though by no means the only one, was that known as 'white lead', a mixture of hydrate and carbonate of lead. A late-eighteenth century source tells us that:

Ceruse is a white calx [burnt residue] of lead, used in painting and cosmetics, made by calcining that metal in the vapour of vinegar. Ceruse is made of thin lamina, or plates of lead, made up into rolls, and so placed as to receive and imbibe the fumes of vinegar contained in a vessel, and set over a moderate fire. The lamina are by means thereof concreted [coalesced] into a white crust, which they gather together, and grinding it up with water form into little cakes. It makes the principal ingredient in the fucuses used by ladies, for the complexion.
Palacocosmos, or the Whole Art of Hairdressing, 1782

The fumes proceeding from this process produced headaches, sickness and even temporary blindness among the people working on it, but even this did not deter the fashionable and wealthy from applying it to their faces. The wearers could expect to suffer from fatigue, heart disease, abdominal pain, gout, kidney failure, joint pain and anaemia; already by the early seventeenth century it was widely believed to cause 'rotting of the teeth and ... unsavoury breath' according to Dr Andreas de Laguna, quoted in *A Treatise against painting and tincturing of Men and Women* (1616).

A much safer recipe was made in medieval times from rosewater and wheat starch, and cyclamen roots were also used. In the eighteenth century, even the wealthy began to turn against white lead, despite the ease with which it could be applied, preferring mixtures based on bismuth (though that was equally toxic), or cuttlefish bone.

A white fucus or beauty for the face

The jaw bones of a hog or sow well burnt, beaten and searced through a fine searce [sieve], and after, ground upon a porphyrie or serpentine stone, is an excellent fucus, being laid on with the oil of white poppy.
Delightes for Ladies to Adorn their Persons, 1636

This basically creates a layer of white calcium phosphate on the skin; ground jaw bones of pigs were a cheaper source for the white face make-up, though the term 'fucus' was applied to colours other than white, and in fact derived from a Latin term applied to red dye.

Mr Wilkinson's ceruse

*On the 18th of June Mr John Wilkinson, of Castle-Head,
Lancashire, obtained a patent for making ceruse or
white lead.*

*Instead of corroding blue lead, by vinegar in pots, with
the heat of dung or bark, Mr Wilkinson takes litharge,
and grinds it exceedingly small in sea-water, or in any
other saline mixture; and then by repeated trituration,
washing and bleaching, he obtains white lead of the best
quality. The saline mixture is used to facilitate the process,
and the ceruse may be procured by levigation, washing
and drying by the medium of the common air, more time
being allowed for the operation.*
Whitehall Evening Post, 5 November 1799

Litharge is an oxide of lead, made by exposing molten
lead to a current of air. Trituration is pulverisation.
Basically this is a paste of powdered white lead oxide in a
saline solution.

There were several ways of creating red colouring for
the face; for the wealthy the safer herbal recipes had less
appeal than imported minerals and grounds. The most
expensive was mercuric sulphide, known as vermilion or
cinnabar, often mixed with lead white, which was known
already in the sixteenth century to loosen teeth and cause
excessive saliva. A safer medieval alternative, Brazilwood,
was noted by Gilbertus Anglicus in 1240, while cheap red
ochre continued to be used into the seventeenth century.
In the mid-nineteenth century carmine, extracted from

cochineal beetles, was still considered safe, but by then was beginning to go out of fashion.

The worst of using rouge is, that one never knows when to stop; women begin by putting on a little, and adding more and more until the whole face is covered with it; the result is anything but pretty.
Beauty and How to Keep it, 'A Professional Beauty', 1889

A water to give the cheeks a carnation colour

Take six ounces of honey, three ounces of isinglass, two ounces of grated nutmegs, and infuse the whole into two quarts of white wine vinegar; distil it over a slow fire, and add to it six grains of red sanders. Before it is used let the lady wash her face with elderflower water, and then her cheeks will assume all the bloom of youth.
The New London Toilet, 1778

The Turkish method of preparing Carmine

Infuse three or four days in a large jar filled with white wine vinegar, a pound of brazil wood shavings of Fernambuca, having first beaten them to a coarse powder; afterwards boil them together about half an hour, then strain off the liquor through a coarse linen cloth, set it again upon the fire, and having dissolved half a pound of alum in white wine vinegar, mix both liquors together, and stir the mixture well with a spatula. The scum that rises is

your carmine, skim it off carefully and dry it for use.
The Toilet of Flora, 1775

Carmine was (and is) a brilliant scarlet powder traditionally obtained from the cochineal beetle, and soluble in ammonia. Cooley (*The Toilet and Cosmetic Arts*, 1866) states that 'so much care, dexterity and patience is required for its successful preparation, as well as a favourable state of the weather, that amateurs seldom attempt it'.

A rouge for the face

Alkanet root strikes a beautiful red when mixed with oils or pomatums. A scarlet or rose coloured ribband wetted with water or brandy, gives the cheeks, if rubbed therewith, a beautiful bloom that can hardly be distinguished from the natural colour. Others only use a red sponge, which tinges the cheeks of a carnation colour.
The Toilet of Flora, 1775

The root of the plant alkanet (*Alkanna tinctoria*) has for centuries been used as a red dye.

Various rouges

Rouge for the complexion: Carmine in fine powder, one part; levigated chalk, five parts. Mix.

Turkish Bloom: Gum benzoin, one pound; powdered red saunders, one and a half pound; dragon's blood, two and half ounces; alcohol, one gallon. Digest for fourteen days, and filter.

Spanish Ladies' Rouge: Take tincture of carmine or cochineal, any quantity, wet some cotton wool with it, and repeat the operation until the wool has sufficient colour.
Toilet Table Talk, 1856

The last of these was the famous 'Spanish wool', which had been in use for centuries. Dragon's blood was a vegetable gum.

Liquid rouge

Several different preparations are sold under this name, but the first of these following only strictly deserves it.

1. Dissolve pure rouge (carthamin) in alcohol, and acidulate the solution with acetic acid. Very rich.

2. A solution of carmine in liquor of ammonia, or in carbonate of potash water, to be diluted for use. Rich coloured.

3. The red liquid left from the preparation of carmine. Inferior to the preceding.

The Toilet and Cosmetic Arts, Arnold Cooley, 1866

Carthamin is the natural red colurant derived since ancient times from safflower. Potassium carbonate, also known as pearl ash and salt of tartar, is used in baking, but is strongly alkaline when dissolved in water.

KEEPING WRINKLES AT BAY

On the subject of wrinkles, the writer of *Beauty and How to Keep it*, 1889 – who styled him- or herself 'A Professional Beauty' – says this: 'Wrinkles – what an ugly word! And to think that they *must* come, sooner or later; but let us try to make it as *late* as possible.'

A pomatum for wrinkles

Take juice of white lily roots and Narbonne honey, of each two ounces, melted white wax an ounce; incorporate the whole together and form thereof a pomatum. It should be applied every night, and not wiped off till the next morning.

Another for the same intention

Take six new laid eggs, boil them hard, take out the yolks and fill the cavities with myrrh and powdered sugar candy, of each equal parts. Join the whites together neatly and set them on a plate before the fire, and mix the liquor that exudes from the whites of eggs with an ounce of hog's-lard. This pomatum must be applied to dry into

the skin, and then the residue wiped off with a clean
fine napkin.
The Toilet of Flora, 1775

Crow's feet

Having once had the privilege of an introduction to a
harem in the East, I was much interested in the sort of
artifice employed by a beauty who was sixty-two years old.
There was no sign of crow's foot on her temples. I was told
that she flattened out the creases by rubbing them out up
and down with her own saliva every morning.
'The Toilet', Mme O de Puy, in *The Ladies' Monthly Magazine*,
1 December 1890

As much as France, the Middle East – and particularly the
harem – was seen as the source of fashionable cosmetics,
with an extra hint of exciting exoticism.

Wrinkles, to smooth and render a charming evenness in the face etc

Take oil of swallows an ounce, oil of mandrake the like
quantity, oil of pomegranate half an ounce, ewes' milk two
ounces, incorporate them over a gentle fire to the thickness
of an ordinary pomatum, then add four ounces of the
cream of sweet almonds.

Spread this thin on a forehead cloth or filleting
[headband], and bind up the forehead pretty straight with

it, and so do several nights, washing it off in the morning with milk or whey mixed with oil of almonds pretty warm; for other parts, where wrinkles appear, lay it on plaster-wise, and it will cause your visage to be smooth and comely.
Beauties Treasury, 1705

Oil of swallows would have been an oil in which the bodies of swallows had been infused.

The cause of wrinkles

When wrinkles are caused by the irreparable outrage of time, and grief, or the vile habit of making grimaces, when laughing or speaking have caused them, they may yet be softened and effaced by degrees, by pressing on them during the night some fine lawn, steeped in gumbenjamin and veal broth, made without either herbs or salt.
The World of Fashion and Continental Feuilletons,
1 October 1827

See page 21 for an earlier recipe using veal to preserve the complexion.

To keep the face without wrinkles

Take an iron frying-pan, and set it on the fire; when it is very hot sprinkle it with good white wine and so fume your face over the smoke thereof, and then wipe it with a clean linen cloth; this done, set the pan on the fire again with

a little myrrh, and with that fume your face as you did
before; whilst you do it cover yourself so that the steam or
smoke may not be dispersed from you; after you have done
this, you tie up your face with some linen cloths, and so go
to bed. This you repeat once in fifteen days.
The Laboratory, or School of Arts, Godfrey Smith, 1738

A water for wrinkles of the face

Take of the decoction of Bryony and figs, each a like
quantity, and wash the face with it. Or take one pomegranate,
hollow it and cleanse it from the inward parts, then infuse
it in whey and wine, each a sufficient quantity, and boil
them till the wine be evaporated; then use it.
Cosmeticks, or the Beautifying Parts of Physick, Johann
Wecker, 1660

The notable aspect of the second recipe is that it uses
the outer parts of the fruit rather than the juice; the
high tannin content in the rind (about twenty per cent)
explains why it has been used as a skin astringent since
classical times.

To take away the wrinkles of the belly
after child bearing

Take of ram's suet, nine times washed in cold water, one
pound, two whites of eggs, a little butter; bruise them all
very well, then add mastic, olibanum, each two drams; mix

them and make an ointment for the belly.
Cosmeticks, or the Beautifying Parts of Physick, Johann
Wecker, 1660

Olibanum is a vegetable gum similar to frankincense.
This ointment would provide protein and oil which would
soften the skin. There is very little evidence that any oils
or creams can prevent stretch marks, but massage, aided
by oils, sometimes helps.

The Gunning sisters

London in the year 1750 witnessed the arrival of two
remarkable sisters from Ireland, Maria and Elizabeth
Gunning; Horace Walpole described them as 'making a
lot of noise'. Their social and marital success was sudden
– within two years Maria was the Countess of Coventry
and Elizabeth the Duchess of Hamilton. Widely praised
for their beauty, they were at the heart of London society,
and were at the vanguard of fashions in clothes and
cosmetics. Elizabeth had a long and successful career,
being the wife to two dukes and the mother of four;
a powerful and clever woman, she died in 1790, of
tuberculosis. Though white lead had ruined her looks
by the age of 30, she had by then been appointed as a
lady of the bedchamber to Queen Charlotte.

Maria early on gained a reputation for enjoying
public attention, and her immaturity and tactlessness

fascinated the writers of the day. Her husband took against her love of make-up, publicly wiping the rouge from her face while the couple were in Paris soon after their marriage. But she persisted, and by the end of the decade she was severely ill from tuberculosis and the effects of excessive use of ceruse (white lead). Her last days were spent lying on a couch with a mirror in her hand, mourning her lost looks. She died in 1760. In 1766 Horace Walpole reported that Lady Fortrose was dying of the same addiction to cosmetics, which the following year killed the celebrated society courtesan Kitty Fisher.

By the 1770s public opinion had begun to turn against heavy make-up in favour of the natural look, and a bill laid before parliament that year proposed to make it illegal to 'betray into matrimony any of his Majesty's subjects by the scents, paints, cosmetic washes, artificial teeth, false hair, Spanish wool … and that the marriage … shall stand null and void'.

A LOVELY FINISH

Horace Walpole (1717–1797) complained that the amount
of face make-up that women wore forced the wearers to
maintain a fixed and emotionless expression. There were
many curious finishes which left little opportunity for
facial movement; the expression 'enamelling the face'
became popular in the nineteenth century.

Enamelling the face

*Enamelling the face and neck is impossible, it never has,
and never can be done. The reason that certain ladies,
not excepting the most illustrious in the land, are stated
to have been enamelled, is because every woman, from
the highest to the lowest, is exposed to the malevolent
tongue of malice, slander and scandal. The slender
base on which these rumours rest is the mere fact that in
some books receipts [recipes] have appeared under the
headings 'Massage enamel' or 'Liquid Enamel', and that
in some cases the preparations contained bismuth salts,
and other metallic preparations. All these drugs must be
more than commercially pure, they must be chemically
pure, otherwise they are cosmetically imperfect, and not
sufficiently fine for cosmetic purposes. The impure salts,*

especially where gas is the usual source of light, change colour on exposure to the air.

Massage Enamel consists of

Bismuth Oxychloride 1 oz., French Chalk 1/2 oz., Putty Powder 1 dr, Soft Paraffin to make 3 oz.

Liquid Enamel is as follows

Bismuth Oxychloride 1 oz., French Chalk 1/2 oz., Putty Powder 1 dr, Water to make 15 oz.

This last preparation might be more accurately described as a liquid face powder. French chalk is a silicate of magnesium, of which talc is another form. In France it is called Venetian talc. Putty powder is oxide of tin – a metal which from its firmness is specially useful for the nails.
The Secrets of Beauty, Cora Brown Potter, 1914

A more or less lost concept now, face enamel was sufficiently outrageous in 1920 to attract the attention of a letter writer to the *Daily Mail* (27 April), who called for a sliding-scale tax on cosmetics with a 'heavy duty on eyebrow pencils, rouge and face enamel'.

A curious varnish for the face

Fill into a bottle three quarters of a pint of good brandy, infuse therein an ounce of gum sandarach, and half an ounce of gum Benjamin, and frequently shake the bottle till the gums are wholly dissolved, then let it stand to settle. Apply this varnish after having washed the face clean, and it will give the skin the finest lustre imaginable.
The Toilet of Flora, 1775

Presumably the wearer would have had to settle on which expression was going to be retained, to avoid cracks appearing.

A composition which gives an admirable lustre to the skin

Take equal quantities of the juice of lemons and of the whites of eggs; beat all together in an earthen pot that is varnished, put it over a gentle fire, and stir it with a wooden spatula till the whole acquires the consistence of butter. Keep it for use, and before you use it you may add to it any perfume that pleases you best. The face is to be washed with rice-water before the application of it. This is one of the best compositions that can be used for rendering the face handsome, bright and smooth.
Abdeker: or, the Art of Preserving Beauty, 1756

Dry Skins

Oatmeal should never be used for them, and soap only once a week; with warm water at bedtime. Instead of soap keep some yolk of egg on your washing-stand, put a little into the palm of your hand, and smear it over your face. If you beat up a fresh yolk with two teaspoons of water, and keep it in a well-stoppered bottle, it will last several days.
Beauty Culture, **H Ellen Browning,** 1898

Pearl powder

*As for the transcendent and divine pearl powder, with an
exquisite varnish superinduced to fix it, it is by no means
common, but is reserved for ladies not only of the first
rank, but of the most considerable fortunes; it being so very
costly, that few pin-moneys can keep a face in it, as a face
of condition ought to be kept. Perhaps the same number of
pearls whole might be more acceptable to some lovers, than
in powder upon the lady's face.*
The Town, 2 January 1755

A deep purse would be required to provide the pearls for
a face powder, so naturally some kind of varnish would
be necessary to keep the powder on. Clearly only for the
super-rich.

A cheaper alternative

*Dr Cook of Leigh, who is as much esteemed for his
philanthropy, as he is celebrated for medical knowledge,
recommends the subjoined prescription as a safe and
excellent cosmetic lotion 'which will set off the countenance
to the best advantage, by rendering an ordinary one
beautiful, and an handsome one more so':*

*Boil two quarts of soft water on four ounces of pure
quicksilver, in an earthen pipkin [bottle], till half the
water is wasted, then pour the water, with the quicksilver
and all, into a bottle to be ready for use: with a fine cloth
dipped into a little of this concoction, wash the face two or*

three times a week in the morning, after having washed as
usual with fresh weater.

It gives a fine lustre to the skin, and cleanses it of all
kinds of foulnesss, as scurfs, insects, morphews, etc, and
is perfectly innocent, and the best deobstruent in physic.
It may be drank freely as a specific against worms; and
against all cutaneous eruptions.

I remember a lady, says he, that has been eminent for
beauty in many courts of Europe, confessed to me that this
insipid liquor was, of all innocent wash for the face, the
best she ever met with.
Hebe; or, the Art of Preserving Beauty, 1786

Quicksilver would give a shine to the face, cheaply emulating
the lustre that ground pearls provided. There would of
course be a different kind of cost.

Tan

Supposing you have just arrived in the south of France, or
wherever it is, and on descending to the plage you
are confronted by a crowd of bronzed and beautiful beings
who make you feel very much like something which has
just crept out from under a stone – what are you going
to do about it? You will go down to the shops, and buy
yourself a bottle of golden-brown liquid make-up with
which you will proceed to anoint your body on every
portion which you propose to exhibit to the public gaze,
allowing, of course, for such contingencies as shrinkage
of bathing suits and suntops that slip a bit.

This make-up is a gift straight from Heaven.
The Way to Beauty, Jane Clare, 1938

And finally

There is a great art in putting on face powder, easy as it seems. Some women have an idea that the thicker it is put on the better it looks! Not at all; this is a great mistake. Powder should be put on the face so lightly and delicately that no one is aware of its presence. There are three shades of face powder, pink, yellow (or Rachel), and white. The first should be used by women of a delicate pink and white complexion, the second by sallow or colourless skins, and the last never, it always shows, and is most unbecoming.
Beauty and How to Keep it, 'A Professional Beauty', 1889

A professional declaration of the demise of white face make-up.

PERFECT SKIN

The quest to find a way of retaining the smooth soft skin of youth lies at the heart of cosmetics; once discovered, such recipes might be kept as closely guarded secrets. *A Discourse of Auxiliary Beauty* (1692) characterised cosmetics as 'many secret medicaments, and close receipts, which may either fill and lump [women's] skins, if flat and wrinkled, or smooth and polish them, if rugged and chapped, or clear and brighten them, if tanned and freckled'.

The Roman physician Galen may have made a cold cream made from wax, oil and water, but cold cream based on lard lasted until the end of the Victorian era.

Cold cream

Lard prepared, two pounds; suet, one pound. Melt, cool a little, and then stir in bergamot, two drachms; essence of lemon, one drachm; neroli, twenty drops; rose-water, four ounces.
Toilet Table Talk, 1856

Neroli is an oil distilled from the flowers of Seville oranges.

A beautifying tincture to preserve a face from the ruins of old age

Take mastic, sandriack, sulphur-vive and ceruse [white face paint] of each two ounces, gum tragacanth three ounces, eggs the whites of them four, blanched almonds two ounces, chamomile flowers half an ounce, bruise and mix them well together with four ounces of oil of tartar, and let them macerate a week or more, then take them out and heat them till they smoke, and press them through a fine thick canvas, and there will come a curious tincture or oil from them, which when you use rub it first gently on the palms of your clean hands, and then with those palms rub it on all parts of your face, neck and breasts, that you would have appear beautiful, and it will cause a curious lustre to appear on the skin, and so fortify it that the injuries of the weather will have not force upon it, and by often using and continuing, it will as it were embalm the skin, keeping it plump and beautiful even to old age.
Beauties Treasury, 1705

Sandriack was sandarac, a vegetable gum. This recipe would create a coating which could not have been good for the skin.

To take away the pock-holes, or any spot in the face

Take white rose-water, and wet a fine cloth therein, and set it all night to freeze, and then lay it upon your face till it be dry; also take three poppies, the reddest you can get, and quarter them, taking out the garbage; then distil them in a quart of new milk from a red cow, and with the water thereof wash your face.

A Closet for Ladies and Gentlewomen, 1611

The marks left by measles or chickenpox, or still more by smallpox, were a feature of many faces before the arrival of vaccination; incidentally, milkmaids' exposure to cowpox explains why many of them escaped smallpox, leading to the much-desired 'milkmaid's complexion'. Possibly the distillation of milk here is an attempt to create the 'essence of milk' as part of the process of vanquishing the effects of smallpox.

John Webster in *The Duchess of Malfi* (1623) was scathing in his observation of how people dealt with the ravages of the smallpox:

There was a lady in France that, having had the small-pox, flayed the skin off her face to make it more level; and whereas before she looked like a nutmeg-grater, after she resembled an abortive hedge-hog.

To take away spots and freckles from the face or hands

The sap that issueth out of a birch tree in great abundance, being opened in March or April with a receiver of glass set under the boring thereof to receive the same, doth perform the same most excellently, and maketh the skin very clear. This sap will dissolve pearl, a secret not known to many.
Delightes for Ladies to Adorn their Persons, 1636

Not very helpful advice perhaps? How many ladies ruined a string of pearls by trying this rather pointless activity? And more to the point, if it dissolves pearl, or mother-of-pearl, what does that indicate it will do to your skin?

A water to whiten freckles and scars of the face

Take of aquavitae four times distilled, three parts, the tops of rosemary flowers two parts, steep them together a day and a night in a vessel well stopped, then distil them.
Cosmeticks, or the Beautifying Parts of Physick, Johann Wecker, 1660

Rosemary flowers are believed to have antioxidant and skin-conditioning properties.

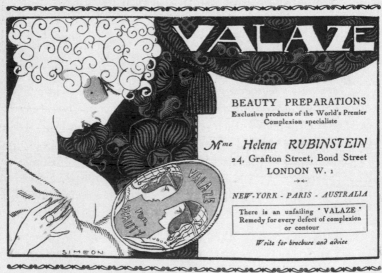

For heat in the face, redness and shining of the nose

Take a fair linen cloth, and in the morning lay it over the grass, and draw it over till it be wet with dew; then wring it out into a fair dish, and wet the face therewith as often as you please; as you wet it let it dry in. May dew is the best.
The Queen's Closet Opened, 1696

The instruction here is to let the moisture seep into the skin; the idea that dew cleanses and moisturises the face beautifully has some reason to it, as dew water would be very pure, especially in rural areas.

A most excellent medicine that the small pox be not seen in the face

When the small pox are cleanly come forth, and that they begin to dry, take Sparma Ceti and warm it in a saucer, and with a feather anoint all the places, often times in the day, as often as it drieth up, that no point of the pox or any other spot shall be seen.
The Queen's Closet Opened, 1696

'Sparma Ceti' was spermaceti, a waxy substance from hunted sperm whales. Effectively this is a hole-filling process; presumably the body's heat kept the spermaceti from drying out and falling off.

A fucus to whiten scars

Take of the roots of orrice, wild cucumbers, each three pound; the roots of marsh mallows, lilies, each two pound; ripe grapes, half a pound; dittander[also known as pepperwort] roots, three ounces; the stalks of beans, pellitory of the wall, each one handful; barley bread, one pound; steep them in white wine or goats' whey [milk], and distil them; then add of radish half an ounce, the four greater cold seeds, each one dram, boy's urine half a pint; set them in the sun and keep them for your use.
The Wit's Cabinet, 1700

Urine alone would probably have done the job. The 'cold seeds' were those of various cucurbitaceous plants, such as marrow and melon.

Fard

This useful paste is good for taking off sun-burnings, effects of weather on the face, and accidental cutaneous eruptions. It must be applied at going to bed. First wash the face with its usual ablution, and when dry, rub this fard all over it, and go to rest with it on the skin. This is excellent for almost constant use.

Take two ounces of sweet almonds, ditto of spermacetti; melt them in a pipkin [bottle] over a slow fire. When they are dissolved and mixed, take it off the fire, and stir into it one table-spoonful of fine honey. Continue stirring till it is cold; and then it is fit for use.
Mirror of the Graces, 1811

'Fard' is a curious word, which became obsolete around 1900. It meant a face paint, especially white.

The use of the flesh-brush to cleanse the skin

The flesh-glove or flesh-rubber of hair is a useful and very convenient modifcation of the flesh-brush. Of these, that known as the 'Indian kheesah' or 'mitten' is superior to all others. For the back, which cannot be easily operated on with the hand, a flat band or belt of hair is employed.

The daily vigorous use of the flesh-brush, or the flesh-glove, for those parts of the body covered with clothing, independent of therapeutic action peculiar to itself, is probably the most healthful, effective, and ready substitute for the entire bath that can be employed under many of the circumstances by which we are frequently surrounded. Occasional personal ablution, or the use of the sponge-bath, after it, greatly increases its good effects.
The Toilet and Cosmetic Arts, Arnold Cooley, 1866

'Dry friction' was intended as an alternative when 'baths or even entire personal ablution cannot be indulged in'; the process was supposed to 'cleanse the skin, excite the cutaneous circulation and invigorate the whole system', and might be carried out 'to any extent short of actual irritation'.

To make the skin, though dusky and brown, as white as alabaster

---

Take oil of tartar an ounce, camphire [camphor] and borax of each a dram, allom [alum] two drams, make these into a fine powder, and put it into a quart of rosewater, with a little handful of rosemary flowers, or rosemary-flower water three ounces, let them simmer half an hour over a gentle fire, then strain it, and keep it close-stopped.

This will whiten the skin so like snow, that the eyes of the beholders will dazzle, if they be fixed too steadfastly upon it.

Beauties Treasury, 1705

How to repair the beauty of an itchy or scabby skin

Take as much mans urine as will serve to bathe the diseased up to the knees; add thereto charcoal of oak powdered, and black hellebore and coal; bathe therewith the legs for fifteen mornings together, and longer if need require. This hath its effect on every member of the body.

Artificial Embellishments, Thomas Jeamson, 1665

For red tawny spots

*In the morning, fasting, chew in the mouth a bit of mastic;
as soon as you perceive it to dissolve anoint the spots
therewith. Or powder pigeons' dung, flax seed, French
barley; soak them in strong vinegar and anoint the spots.*
Artificial Embellishments, Thomas Jeamson, 1665

Pigeons' dung contains acids and ammonia, which when
dried and then exposed to moisture – further acid in the
case of strong vinegar – can be quite corrosive; its effects
on metal are much feared. Despite the emollient powers
of the grain, this mix could potentially burn delicate skin.

A snail-pomatum

*Take as many snails as you please, and beat them in
a mortar with a sufficient quantity of the oil of sweet
almonds; strain by expression, and add an ounce of virgin-
wax for every four ounces of oil. Wash the whole in the
water of frog's-spawn, and add a few drops of the essence
of lemons, in order to correct the bad smell.*
Abdeker: or, the Art of Preserving Beauty, 1756

Vanishing cream

*Vanishing creams of the nourishing variety are the best
used in conjunction with a superfine powder and cream
rouge. In some cases it is better to cut out washing with*

soap and water altogether and to cleanse with a cold or liquefying cream or complexion milk, but individual dry skins which are not hypersensitive may be washed with soft water and superfatted soap with no ill-effects. The best way to preserve a dry skin is to treat it nightly with skin-food, oil or a really reliable Hormone cream.
The Way to Beauty, Jane Clare, 1938

Among those recommended were Mdme. Pomeroy's Skin Food ('made from a very old recipe'), Marguerite Hoare Lettuce Foundation Cream ('pale green foundation cream made from fresh lettuce') and Kathleen Court Facial Youth Cream ('Contains a special medicated clay all the way from New Zealand'). Superfatted soaps contained lanolin, allowing them to 'overcome the action of free alkali' (Sonya Jolsen).

Skin food

Casein, which is found in milk, is an easily obtained skin food. Ordinary milk cream supplies this form of external nourishment. Only a very small quantity is necessary. Apply the cream during the daytime. It is inadvisable to leave this skin food on the face all night because uncooked milk products attract germs and quickly become rancid. Allow the milk cream to remain on the face about two or three hours and then remove it completely.
The Way to Beauty; a complete guide to personal loveliness, Sonya Jolsen, 1937

An excellent pomatum to clear the skin

*Wash barrow's grease [boar's grease] often-times in May-
dew that hath been clarified in the sun, till it be exceeding
white; then take marsh-mallow roots, scraping off the
outsides; then make thin slices of them, and mix them; set
them to macerate in a seething balneo [bain marie], and
scum it well till it be thoroughly clarified and will come to
rope; then strain it and put now and then a drop of May-
dew therein, beating it till it be thorough cold in often
change of May-dew; then throw away that dew, and put
it in a glass, covering it with May-dew; and so reserve it to
your use. Let the mallow roots be two or three days dried
in the shade before you use them. This I had of a great
professor of art, and for a rare and dainty secret, as the
best fucus this day in use.*
Delightes for Ladies to Adorn their Persons, 1636

The roots of mallow secrete a gum, which when boiled
becomes viscid and stringy when lifted. May dew,
collected in May, most desirably on May Day, was long
thought to have special medical and cosmetic properties.
The repeated refining process in this recipe, using a liquid
already thought to be pure, shows an ambition to produce
a very 'dainty' cosmetic cream.

A sweet and delicate pomander

*Take two ounces of labdanum; of benjamin and storax, one
ounce; musk, six grains; civet, six grains; amber-grease, six*

grains; of calamus aromaticus and lignum aloes, of each the
weight of a groat; beat all these in a hot mortar and with an
hot pestle, till they come to paste; then wet your hand with
rosewater, and roll up the paste suddenly [promptly].
Delightes for Ladies to Adorn their Persons, 1636

Labdanum was a fragrant vegetable gum, as were
benjamin and storax; 'amber-grease' was a common
spelling of 'ambergris'. *Calamus aromaticus* was possibly
sweet-scented lemongrass, and lignum aloes was by this
time the term for a scented wood from Mexico. The
gentle heat would have allowed the ingredients to melt
and merge without burning. The pomander would have
been used to create a pleasant smell close to the body, to
both create an aura of fragrance and ward off supposedly
airborne disease evidenced by bad smells.

Orange-flower Pomatum

Take two pounds and a half of hog's-lard, and three
pounds of orange flowers; mix them together in a marble
mortar; then put the mixture into an earthenware vessel
with some water, and place it in a vapour bath, where let
it stand till the lard is melted and floats above the flowers.
When it has stood cold, pour away the water, and simmer
in the same manner as before, with three pounds of fresh
orange-flowers; repeat the same operation twice more with
two pounds of orange-flowers each time, and the last time,
while the mixture stands in infusion, add a gill of orange-
flower water. Strain through an hair sieve held over an

earthenware dish, drain off the water thoroughly when cold, and keep in a dry place in a gallypot closely tied over with a bladder till wanted.
The Toilet of Flora, 1775

A similar recipe in the same book uses apples, melons and cucumber in place of orange flowers. In either case the ingredients were not cheap.

An oil for ringworm in the face

Take a green live lizard, boil it in wine and oil, till the wine be consumed, then strain and use it.
Cosmeticks, or the Beautifying Parts of Physick, Johann Wecker, 1660

There might be some protein in this, but it would not have any specific effect on ringworm, which is caused by a fungal infection.

See-through skin

For many centuries the idea of the perfect skin was that it should give the impression of a slight translucence, or even transparency, as if 'clear skin' was not just clear of blemishes, but literally see-through. Charlotte, the daughter of Elizabeth Gunning, complained of

Princess Charlotte in 1809 that her skin was 'white, but not a transparent white', while Lord Byron's skin was praised for being almost translucent.

Portraits of Queen Elizabeth and a number of aristocratic women living around 1600 show blue veins painted on temples, hands and breasts: in John Marston's *The Malcontent* (1603) Maquerelle refers to 'Doctor Plaster-face' who 'is the most exquisite in forging of veins ... blushing of cheeks, surphling [washing] of breasts, blanching and bleaching of teeth, that ever made an old lady gracious by torchlight'. A poem by William Herbert, 'A Paradox in Praise of a Painted Woman' (1660), includes the lines:

Do not I know those Balls of blushing red
Which on thy Cheeks thus amorously be spread;
Thy sinewy neck, those veins upon thy brow,
Which with their azure winkles sweetly bow,
Are artfull borrowed, and no more thine own
Than chains which on Saint George's day are shown
Are proper to the wearer ...

This clearly indicates that veins were painted on.

The process was again in use in the 1730s and the 1860s; in every case the implication is towards transparency of the skin. Face varnishes and enamelling in the eighteenth and nineteenth centuries used ingredients such as gums and brandy or egg-white which would keep the face rigid, and giving the appearance of a semi-transparent surface.

HAIR – THE CROWNING GLORY

The rigid military training of the ancient Spartans was relaxed in one aspect – in wartime they were encouraged to wear their hair long. Throughout history, probably no aspect of the body has been 'beautified' to such extremes more than our hair.

CARE

To avoid baldness

When it occurs in persons of or under the middle age, and apparently enjoying good health, it may be often traced to the pernicious practice of constantly wearing a hard non-ventilating hat, or to a disordered stomach or liver, habitual smoking or hard drinking, irregular habits, late hours, or the like. Excessive anxiety or grief, and intense study or thoughtfulness, also tend to promote the early loss and decay of the hair.
The Toilet and Cosmetic Arts, Arnold Cooley, 1866

Cooley particularly blamed 'waterproof clothing and silk-hats, and the very general use of tobacco by the juvenile and scarcely mature portion of our population'.

Some hair treatments

A water to make the hair grow: Take of the flesh of snails, wasps, bees, horseleeches, burnt salt, each a like quantity; put them in a glazed vessel, having small holes at the bottom like a sieve, and put under that another glazed vessel which may receive the moisture which will drop forth in many days by degrees. Take that and rub the places that have no hair with it.

'In many days'; the smell must have been fairly potent.

A water against shedding the hair: Take of pure honey, candy wine, a boy's urine, milk, each one pint, and distil a water with which you must wash the places from whence the hairs fall.

Another, more effectual: Take of mountain hyssop, mountain calamint, the leaves of southernwood, each two handfuls; rich candy wine, piss, honey, milk, each two pints; mustard-seed, half a pound. Powder those things which ought to be, then mix them, and let them steep three days; afterwards distil the water, the use of which will suddenly bring forth a beard, and restore hair to bald places.
Cosmeticks, or the Beautifying Parts of Physick, Johann Wecker, 1660

The second was obviously to be applied judiciously; a spillage could have unwanted consequences.

To preserve the hair from falling off

Burn pigeons' dung to ashes, of which take the quantity of an ounce; put them into water where wood-ashes have soaked; then add two ounces of the juice of houseleek, and one of sugar candy, and half an ounce of rosemary flowers; boil them together, strain them well, and wash the place six or seven times, and the hair will not only remain firm, but what is fallen off will renew.

The Accomplished Ladies Rich Closet of Rarities, 1687

To lengthen the hair

Hair, though an excrement, is yet cherished as a plant of value; for most fancy it to be the microcosmical flax whereof Cupid twists his bowstrings. To see it (I confess) in the female sex of a more than usual length is a pleasing spectacle, and if there be any Lady that desire it, she may by these means effect her wishes.

Take old white lard, three pound, mince and beat it till it come to a paste, then distil it in an alembic, and keep the water that arises from it to anoint the hair. It will make the hair of a fair length and soft.

Artificial Embellishments, Thomas Jeamson, 1665

Some residual nourishment from the distilled lard might help the hair follicles, but of likely more benefit would be the removal of impurities in the distillation process, providing a clean liquid for washing the scalp. However, the age of the lard is of some concern.

A powder to prevent baldness

*Powder your head with powdered parsley seed, three
nights every year, and the hair will never fall off.*
The Toilet of Flora, 1775

The ubiquitous lard would have been used to keep the
powder in place, and might have helped.

A compound oil to quicken the growth of hair

*Take half a pound of green southernwood bruised, boil
it in a pint and a half of sweet oil and half a pint of
red wine; when sufficiently boiled remove it from the fire,
and strain off the liquor through a linen bag; repeat this
operation three times with fresh southernwood; the last
time add to the strained liquor two ounces of bears-grease.*
The Toilet of Flora, 1775

Bears' grease — a fat obtained from dead bears — was a
much favoured ingredient in hair restorers.

An oil to preserve and increase the hair

*Take the seeds of marsh-mallows, a sufficient quantity;
boil them in common oil, with which anoint the hairs. Also
the oil of earth-worms doth increase the hair.*
**Cosmeticks, or the Beautifying Parts of Physick, Johann
Wecker, 1660**

The seeds of marsh mallow were not often used; the roots, leaves and flowers were used historically as a treatment for inflammation. Current research suggests that earthworms may have antibacterial properties; a healthy scalp might help hair growth.

To take away hair

Take the shells of fifty-two eggs, beat them small, and distil them with a good fire, and with the water anoint yourself where you would have the hair off; or else cats-dung that is hard and dried, beaten to a powder, and tempered with strong vinegar, and anointed on the place.
The Queen's Closet Opened, 1696

'Tempering' here involved mixing with vinegar. Despite the cost and work involved it is difficult to imagine many people deciding not to prefer the first option, no matter how many eggs were involved.

To make the hair of the beard to grow

Take cane roots, briony roots, beets, radish, flower de luce [iris], onions, of each alike the quantity of four ounces, six fat figs bruised and stamped very small, maidenhair, southernwood, dill, of each a handful; seethe all these in good wine, then wring out the liquor and strain it through a strainer, then put to it fresh butter never salted, pure honey two ounces, oil of almonds sweet and sour,

oil of sefania an ounce, orimell squillick half an ounce,
the powder of meal, nigella, fenugreek, well sifted and
thoroughly boulted in a boulter [sieve], one handful of
'Grasse Labeanum'; set these upon the fire and stir them
well till it be thick. This linament being applied to the chin
and cheeks will become hair; the body first purged from all
filth inwardly. Proved by experience.
The Widow's Treasure, 1595

'Grasse Labeanum' may be labdanum wax. 'Oil of sefania' may be from the no-longer identifiable plant known in the sixteenth century as 'siphany'; 'oximell squillick' was probably 'oximel of squills', a drink made from vinegar and honey, in which bulbs of the sea-onion were infused. This recipe promises a magical transformation, though quite what it was doing in a book for widows is not clear.

An ointment to restore the hair

Lay upon the hair burnt bees mixed with honey. Or take
the roughest foam of the sea burnt, and powdered and
smoothed with oil, lay it on the place, but especially let
it be lamp oil. Or the shells of sea hedgehogs burnt, and
wrought together with bears-grease, lay it upon the places,
being first rubbed.
Cosmeticks, or the Beautifying Parts of Physick, Johann
Wecker, 1660

The image of gathering sea-foam and burning it is bizarre and exciting; presumably some minerals would be extracted. The lamp oil specified would have been whale oil, a very fine oil, which may have aided penetration through the skin. Honey's antiseptic qualities may have helped in cases of hair loss caused through skin infection.

Ointments against an old baldness

Take of sea-hedge-hogs burnt together with their shells, unripe galls, bitter almonds burnt, each two ounces; mouse-turd one dram; powder them well and dissolve them in vinegar, and lay them on.

Take the hairs of a bear burnt, maidenhair burnt, the roots of reeds burnt, shreds of haircloth burnt, each equal parts; mix it up with bears-grease and rosin of cedar-tree.
Cosmeticks, or the Beautifying Parts of Physick, Johann Wecker, 1660

Bear's grease was still popular in Victorian times, while haircloth was indeed cloth made of hair from horses, cows and other animals – rather than human hair. The outlandish nature of some of the ingredients says a lot about the desperation attendant upon baldness.

Ointments to hinder the growth of hair

Take of ants' eggs, the blood of frogs, the rust of iron, mix them up with spittle.

Take the gall of a hedgehog, the gall of a cormorant, sea-shells burnt and powdered, the blood of a bat, each a sufficient quantity; make an ointment.

   *Take of burnt dates two drams, spike [French lavender]
one dram and a half; powder and mix them with honey,
and the turd of a mole, to the form of an unguent.*
**Cosmeticks, or the Beautifying Parts of Physick, Johann
Wecker, 1660**

Acquiring the galls of a hedgehog and a cormorant must
have taken some diligence. Similar diligence is required
to find any efficacious materials in these recipes, though
honey would probably have done no harm.

To take away the hair

*Take of the powder of an owl one ounce, cummin, the
blood of a bat, each three ounces, musk, one scruple; make
a linament; we must have a special care that the part to
which the ointment must be applied be first washed with a
lye made of vine ashes, and if an itching be left in the part
after application of the medicine, anoint it with radishes,
white ointment, or with the decocotion of henbane-seeds, or
of colewort seeds.*
**Cosmeticks, or the Beautifying Parts of Physick, Johann
Wecker, 1660**

Clearly this remedy had been used, and note taken of its
effects. 'The powder of an owl' may have been crushed owl
pellets, rather than 'powdered owl'. A lye was an alkaline
liquid, often made by mixing wood-ash with water.

Two remedies for split ends

Hair that is very slender, when by Nature it is spun to its utmost length, must be well regarded and carefully kept, or by sundry accidents it will be frayed and ravelled at the ends, which seem to envy that work they cannot mend; then take as a provision against such injuries these instructions; mix oil of roses and water a like quantity, anoint the hair with it going to bed, and turn it up against the next morning; boil the bark of a willow tree, fleabane and marshmallows, in running water, and wash your head with the decoction.

The Ladies Dictionary, 1694

When you go to bed take oil and water, a like quantity, put them into a bottle, incorporate them well together; anoint the hair well with it on going to bed; next morning wash it with this following: take marsh mallows, fleabane, and willow-bark, boil them in spring water, and use it to wash the head. This will keep the hair from splitting, but if it be split already you must use this:

Take myrtle and willow leaves, of each two ounces; powdered ladbanum six scruples; emblic myrobalans, powdered, half a dram; white wine two ounces. Boil all these over a gentle fire to a consumption of the third part of it, then use to anoint the extremities of the hair therewith.

Artificial Embellishments, Thomas Jeamson, 1665

It is difficult to know how the second formula would work; presumably it was intended to stop further splitting of affected locks, rather than knit the strands together again. Neither myrtle nor willow leaves are well known now for treatment of split ends, which are mainly found in dry hair – but the oil would have been a good basic treatment. The use of marsh mallows, fleabane and willow bark in both recipes suggests that these were then well known and widely used ingredients for this complaint. Myrobalan, sometimes called emblic myrobalan, is a plum-like fruit, with astringent qualities, formerly used medicinally, but now more as source for dyes.

DESIGN

Waving hair

The French furriers and felt-manufacturers have a method called 'sécrétage' for waving hair, a modified form of which is sometimes applied to living human hair, but the process is extremely dangerous ...

The process involves the hair being moistened with the liquid for half of its length, care being taken that the liquid did not touch the skin. The hair could be set in position in waves or curls for a few hours before being washed, and the design would set for up to three weeks.

The danger in this operation is the corrosive character of the sécrétage liquid which is composed of one drachm of quicksilver dissolved in two ounces of nitric acid. Before use it is diluted with half its volume of water. It has been applied to vigorous hair without immediately harmful results; but there are instances where it has

produced most unpleasant and disastrous consequences;
and it can never be considered as other than an extremely
hazardous operation.
The Woman Beautiful, Adelia Fletcher, 1899

'Permanent waves' began around this time, but clearly the
first experiments were hazardous. The word 'perm' is not
documented until as late as 1925.

To curl the hair

Take three ounces of pine-nut kernels, dry them and beat
them to a powder, and then add to them half a pint of
water of wall-flowers, and two ounces of the oil of myrtle;
boil them into a thickness, and straining out the liquid part,
anoint the hair and roll it up; and so you will find it will, in
twice or thrice doing keep the curl.
The Accomplished Ladies Rich Closet of Rarities, 1687

Worth a try?

How to make the hair curl

Twining curls are now much the mode, and none thought
paragons for Beauty save those whose graceful locks do
reach the breasts and make spectators think those ivory
globes of Venus are upheld by the friendly aid of their
crispy twirls. If any affect the fashion they may serve
themselves with these directions so advantageously that

Fig. 95
WAVING THE SECOND STRAND

*none shall desire to be free that may have the glory to be
fettered with their curled hair.*

*Some to make their hair curl wind it up going to bed
upon a hot tobacco pipe or iron. Others dissolve gum
arabic or mouth glue in water, moistening the hair with
it; afterwards they let it dry. Some instead thereof use the
white of an egg or else beer or ale. But to give you farther
and better directions, first rub the hair with lye [strong
alkaline solution] or urine, so that it may be washed very
clean; then take 20 oak galls, maidenhair two ounces, and
as much salt water, boiled to the consistency of honey,*

work them well together, and for two days anoint the hair
therewith; on the third day wash it with this following bath:
Boil fern roots, beet leaves, of each a like quantity, so
long in water till a third part of the water be consumed;
then take it from the fire, put in a little gum arabic and
when it is cool use it.
Artificial Embellishments, Thomas Jeamson, 1665

The early version of curling tongs was clearly a warm pipe
or heated metal rod, but which of the ingredients would
help the hair curl? Gerard's *Herbal* says of maidenhair
that it 'maketh the hair of the head or beard to grow
that is fallen and pulled off', while oak galls are a well
known black hair dye. Bracken has been used to promote
hair growth, and Culpeper stated that beet juice 'is much
commended against baldness and shedding the hair'. All
in all these may have helped preserve the strength and
health of the hair while it was being heated on an iron bar
or washed in urine.

Gum arabic added to the final wash would fix the hair
in whatever shape it was placed.

To make the hair lank and flag

The bushy forest of the head is sometimes labyrinthed
with mazy and rude meanders, while the locks themselves
retreat in such recoiling twirls as if they took the breasts for
a pair of snowy mountains, and were afraid their tender tops
should touch them; they may be forced to extend themselves to
a pleasing length if you follow these prescriptions.

Take borage and mallows, beat them small and work them well together with common oil, let them stand together in a warm place a day and a night; next morning put them in an alembic, and distil them over a gentle fire. The water that you draw from them keeps the hair from frisling and makes it flag and smooth.
Artificial Embellishments, Thomas Jeamson, 1665

'Flag' here means 'hang down'; 'frisling' is a lovely word, meaning 'forming into tight curls'. Distillation in an alembic would produce a liquid free from impurities. Mallow is said to support moisture balance within the hair, while borage is supposed to maintain healthy hair. Herbs used to straighten hair usually are selected on the basis of their moisturising properties, assuming that dry hair is more likely to 'frisle', so borage at least may be appropriate.

Ointment to curl the hair

Take a sufficient quantity of ram's horns, cut it and powder it with oil, and anoint the hair.
Cosmeticks, or the Beautifying Parts of Physick, Johann Wecker, 1660

Pre-modern medicine often applied the 'theory of signatures'; the idea that things were placed on Earth as remedies for diseases, and could be recognised by 'signs' which pointed out their similarity to the issue to be resolved. The use of the curling ram's horn seems to be one of these cases.

Macassar oil

*There is, in fact, no such thing imported into the country,
although many thousands of pounds are annually
expended, both in the advertising and the purchase of an
article which passes under the name. The ingredients of
which it is composed are the most simple and economical.
The following is the genuine recipe:-*

Take:-

3 quarts of common oil,

1/2 pint of spirits of wine,

3 ounces of cinnamon powder,

2 ounces of bergamot.

*Beat them together in a large pipkin [bottle]. Then
remove it from the fire; add four small pieces of alkanet
root, and keep it closely covered for several hours; let it
them be filtered through a funnel lined with filtering paper.*

Beauty's Mirror, 1839

'Macassar Oil', made by Rowland and Sons, is believed
to have been made from ingredients from Makassar, in
Indonesia. There was also a macassar poison and a macassar
wood, possibly causing the confusion here alluded to.
Macassar oil was used by nineteenth-century gentlemen
to such an extent that cloths called anti-macassars were
used to protect the backs of armchairs. It was so famous
that it made its way into Byron's *Don Juan*, with the note
'see the advertisement'.

In virtues nothing could surpass her,
Save thine "incomparable oil", Macassar!

For a soft beard

This following makes a soft beard, and doth beautify the chin with a fine haire. Take butter without salt, the juyce of a red onion, the grease of a gray or a badger, the roote of bryony, of beet, of radish, and of whyte lilies: whereof make a linament, and annoint the chin often therewith, being shaven.
A Thousand Notable Things, **Thomas Lupton, 1579**

A 'gray' was a Eurasian badger, with grey fur. Lupton took his recipe from Mizaldus, a sixteenth-century French doctor and astrologer. It is unclear how this would work – presumably by softening the hairs as they grow.

Hair spray

It is most refreshing to have the hair sprayed with a scented solution of either spirit or vinegar. After this has been done the head is fanned with either a hand or electric fan, to promote the evaporation of the spray. Bay-rum is the best preparation for spraying the hair. The best bay-rum is made from the fresh leaves and berries in the West Indies; it can, however, be made anywhere, but as the process is exceedingly difficult and requires distillation and redistillation, I have not given any receipt. It will be found better and cheaper to buy it from a recognised chemist.
The Secrets of Beauty, **Cora Brown Potter, 1914**

After centuries of home-made recipes at last we are given refreshing permission to just go shopping. Quite how much the smell of scented vinegar would be refreshing is open to question.

To soften the hair when too harsh and stiff

The hair on some hangs like thatch on a country cottage, and serves more for use than ornament, to secure them from the impetuous injuries of wind and weather, rather than with its soft and tender sleeves to delight admiring eyes. Such stiff bristles are usual attendants to churlish Corydons, who are represented by nothing better than the parallel emblem of surly swine. Those then who desire a more graceful covering, and would alter the harsh conceit that others are apt to entertain of their hoggish natures, may to their great advantage use these directions.

Take newts' eggs, henbane seed, rock alum, psyllium and opium, of each a like quantity, boil them in distilled water of vinegar; bathe the hair well therewith; when you have done this, make this powder: take salt nitre four ounces, pumice stone powdered two ounces, lily roots and cuttle bone, of each two drams; beat them all very fine and rub the hair with it. After you have done this use again the former decoction.

Artificial Embellishments, Thomas Jeamson, 1665

'Corydon' was a generic name for a rustic character in pastoral poetry. Psyllium is a name given to several members of the plantain family, while opium is well known, by reputation if not experience. What is curious here is the alternate use of newts' eggs, which are fairly gelatinous, and powdered pumice and cuttle bone, which, though high in calcium, would also cause damage to the hair by being rubbed in.

BRUSHING, WASHING AND DRESSING THE HAIR

Brushing the hair

Perfect cleanliness is indispensable for the preservation of the hair's beauty and colour, as well as its duration; it should be washed frequently in tepid soft water, using soaps which have the smallest portion of alkali in their composition. After washing, the hair should be thoroughly dried, and then well brushed, until its lightness and elasticity are restored; in dressing it, a little marrow pomatum, bear's-grease, or fragrant oil, should be sparingly used. The constant use of the brush is a great means of beautifying, renders the hair glossy and elastic, and encourages a disposition to curl.
Toilet Table Talk, 1856

Arnold Cooley, in *The Toilet and Cosmetic Arts* (1866), recommended that 'very rough, coarse, scratching brushes, carelessly used, are a fertile sourse of injury to the hair and skin of the head.' The tendency to brush the crown and parting areas of the head would lead to premature baldness: 'No scalp and no hair, however healthy and

vigorous, can long stand, without injury, the irritation and strain to which they are thus subjected.'

Washing the hair

Personally I am not a great advocate of hairwashing at home, unless you have a very experienced maid to do it, and every convenience for doing it well. It is far better, in the majority of cases, to go to a good hairdresser and let him do it for you once in every four or five weeks; but be sure you make him dry it thoroughly, by rubbing the scalp, before he toasts your long hair with the patent machine that invariably reminds me of an improved up-to-date dutch-oven. Otherwise you will probably suffer from a form of nervous or rheumatic pain in the back of the head afterwards.
Beauty Culture, H Ellen Browning, 1898

Anything resembling a dutch-oven (essentially a radiating hot-plate) must have been a very risky thing to put near your hair.

An oil scented with flowers for the hair

Salad oil, oil of sweet almonds, and oil of nuts are the only ones made use of for scenting the hair.
Blanch your almonds in hot water, and when dry, reduce them to powder, sift them through a fine sieve, strow a thin bed of almond powder and a bed of flowers over the bottom of a box lined with tin, and do this alternately

*till the box is full. Leave them together from morning
till night, then throw away the flowers and add fresh
ones in the same manner as before, and repeat the same
operation every day for eight successive days. When the
almond powder is thoroughly impregnated with the scent
of the flower made choice of, put it into a new clean linen
cloth, and with an iron press extract the oil, which will be
strongly scented with the fragrant perfume of the flower.*
The Toilet of Flora, 1775

A delightful-sounding recipe, and one which is unlikely
to do the hair any harm.

Pomatum for the hair

*Cut a quantity of hog's cheek into small pieces, steep it six or
eight days in clean water, which must be changed three times
a day; and every time the water is changed, let the flesh be
stirred with a spatula, or the shank of a silver table-spoon;
strain the flesh dry, and put it in a clear earthen pipkin
[bottle] with a pint of rose-water, and a lemon stuck with
cloves; simmer them over the fire till the scum looks reddish,
which take off; remove the pipkin from the fire, and strain
the liquor. When it has cooled, take off the fat, beat it several
times well with cold water, till thoroughly purified, using
rose-water the last time instead of common water; drain the
pomatum from the water, and scent it with any perfume to
your choice, such as essence of bergamot, lemon, etc.*

*This is an elegant and excellent composition for almost
every cosmetic purpose; but particularly for the hair, which*

it nourishes, strengthens, preserves, and thickens; and in
that respect it seems a natural pabulum or food.
Hebe; or, the Art of Preserving Beauty, 1736

The first soaking process presumably cleans the fatty
flesh, which is then simmered with rose-water, lemon and
cloves. After removing the scum and straining the liquor,
there would be a layer of fat floating on the top, and this is
again beaten with water, drained and mixed with perfume.
Essentially the result is purified and scented lard.

Bears' grease

An imaginary, or at least, greatly exaggerated, notion of
the efficacy of this grease exists. People are, however, now
becoming a little less confident of its merits than they were
a few years since. To those, however, who are in the habit of
purchasing it, the following information may be acceptable.
It consists of two sorts – one, about the consistency of fine oil,
which is produced by boiling, from the fat about the caul and
intestines of the bear; the other is harder, and obtained from
about the kidneys. The smell of both is unpleasant and rancid.
Beauty's Mirror, 1839

Bears' grease, which had long been used as the basis for
skin creams, was in the nineteenth century hailed as
an excellent hair restorer and promoter of hair growth.
Expensively imported, and in limited supply, it became
difficult to obtain and very expensive. Nevertheless,
it was still felt at this time that there was not really an

When Illness puerile makes the Hair,
What is it gives it strength,
Restores the grace that decks the Fair,
Improves its tone and length.
Those who have felt this woeful loss
Answer - tis Bears Grease - sold by ROSS.

alternative to bears' grease, particularly as a base for hair pomade. Victorian gentlemen's whiskers particularly benefited from lavish applications of bear's grease.

COLOUR

Black lead for the hair

Black lead combs do very well for ladies who have grey hair, and never wear powder, but then they must be used very carefully, not runned too often in one place, for fear you should black it in shades, or make it look streaked, but this method is attended with a deal of trouble, and not without some injury to the hair.
The Art of Hair-dressing, and Making it Grow Fast, William Moore, 1750

This would be lead ore or metallic lead – indeed not good for the hair, though it would make it shiny temporarily.

An oil to black the hair

Oil made of green lizards doth black the hair. Or take of privet, vitriol, common oil, each a sufficient quantity, set them to the fire till they begin to boil, and keep it to anoint the hair. Or take an hundred green nuts, common oil a pint and a half, liquid alum three pounds; put all these together into a new earthenware vessel first made wet, and being carefully anointed about set it in a place not too moist and

*not too hot, and let it be under the earth three months, then
take it away and use the oil.*
Cosmeticks, or the Beautifying Parts of Physick, Johann
Wecker, 1660

The lizard in question was probably the common wall
lizard *Podarcis muralis*, which is sometimes found with a
greenish skin colouration. Black walnuts have been used
as a source of black dye for centuries.

To make hair as yellow as gold

*Take the rind or scrapings of rhubarb, and steep it in white
wine, or in clear lye. And after you have washed your head
with it, you shall wet your hairs with syringe or some
other cloth, and let them dry by the fire or in the sun. After
this, wet them and dry them again, for the oftener they
do it, the fairer they will be, without hurting your head
anything at all.*
The Treasurie of Commodious Conceits, 1584

This would have been dried rhubarb, as the plant was not
grown from seed in Britain until 1777.

To make the hair yellow

*If any Lady be in love with this colour she may order her
hair thus: take shavings of box, stechas [French lavender],
cedar, liquorice roots scraped and bruised, coltsfoot roots,*

maidenhair, of each two ounces, and a little saffron. Set all
these over the fire till two parts of the water be consumed,
then strain it, and wash the hair therewith.

Or take the first buds of the black poplar, pound them
with fresh butter, set them in the sun for five days, then
strain them and press out the butter, wash it with lye made
from the ashes of box tree, then use it to anoint the hair.
Artificial Embellishments, Thomas Jeamson, 1665

It seems gentlemen have been preferring blondes for
centuries. Early medieval texts indicate the desire for
yellow hair, red lips, white skin and eyebrows dyed black.

A water to make the hair red

Take of the water of radish, of privet as much as
sufficient, mix them and wash the hair.

A water to make the hair white

Take of the greater centaury four ounces, the lees of
alum eight ounces, rock-alum and gum arabic, each two
ounces, clean white soap and gum tragacanth and water,
six ounces; boil them to one half and strain it, and the head
being washed with it, and dried by the sun, last of all wash
it with lye.
Cosmeticks, or the Beautifying Parts of Physick, Johann
Wecker, 1660

A lye to make the hair fair

If you would have your hair fair, and sweet scented, wash your head with Galons lye, called 'the distilled lye', which is made of a little ash of a vine burnt, of the knots of barley straw, and liquorice, sow-bread; and while the head is combed sprinkle the hair with the powder of cloves, roses, nutmeg, cardamom and galingale, with rose-water, dipping the comb also into it; also they are made fair being often washed with the decoction of beech-tree nuts.
Cosmeticks, or the Beautifying Parts of Physick, Johann Wecker, 1660

Sow-bread was the name given to a kind of cyclamen, whose tuberous roots were favoured by pigs.

Of ointment that will dye the hair white

Take of swallows' dung, the gall of a bull, each a sufficient quantity; mix them and make an ointment.
Cosmeticks, or the Beautifying Parts of Physick, Johann Wecker, 1660

Presumably a 'sufficient quantity' would be enough to work into the entire head. The sensation must have been interesting.

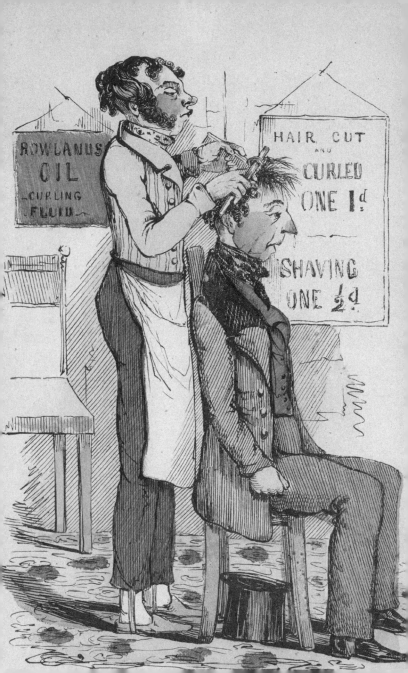

FALSE HAIR

False hair in the eighteenth century meant elaborate hair constructions coated with lard and powder. Lard thickened the hair and provided a hold for the powder, which was blown on with 'powder machines' – bellows or syringes. The hair constructions were sometimes so high that they often constituted a fire hazard as they knocked into chandeliers.

In 1721, the Friends' meeting at Hampton, Massachusetts determined that 'the wearing of extravagent wigges is altogether antagonistic to truth'.

Of the various fashions of dressing the hair; and first, of a small toupee

The smooth toupee may be considered as one of the first modern fashions of dressing ladies hair; and though there is now a great variety, yet still some prefer it before any other, as it is allowed to hurt the hair the least of any, and may be dressed very becoming to many ladies whose hair is of a glossy colour, and grows regularly round the face. It may be dressed in different forms, and ought to be without powder, for that gives it a rusty look: one or two curls at each ear will give it a grace; and if a little cap is to be worn with it, it should be round at the top of the head; and some it will suit to wear in the form of a heart, as by that means a seat will be left for the cap: and to make it appear more dressed, curls may be placed on the sides of the toupee, till they touch the cap, in one or two rows of

curls, according to fancy. This method of dressing the hair will not stay so long in dress as some others, but it is much sooner done, and easier for the hair.
A Treatise on the Hair, David Ritchie, 1770

There were names for the specific kinds of curls: a 'confidant' was a small curl next to the ear, a 'creve-coeur', also called a 'heart-breaker', was a curled lock at the nape of the neck, and 'all-favourites' hung down at the temples (*The Ladies Dictionary*, 1694).

Tetes

Tetes are made like the hair and should be brought exact where it grew, that they may be the more natural; the fronts are not to be seen to appear like a wig, but the crape hair, which is round the edges, should be adjusted and lay as close as possible by using a little pomatum. Ladies who wear a braid, or cushion in the pole, sometimes have curls fastened to the sides of the cushion; long hair braids are fixed between the hair with a small pole-comb, and to make it more secure you may run a string, or long pin up the cushion, turn it back; the string may be pinned at the back of the cushion. Curls fastened on the toupee may be worn at the sides, or done on wire, fastened to the cushion, or toupee; these methods all depend on fancy.
The Art of Hair-dressing, and Making it Grow Fast, William Moore, 1750

Moore describes himself as 'ladies Hair-dresser and Perfumer, (Red House), Orange Grove, Bath', where his book was published. He was an enthusiastic proponent of good-quality materials, including hair powder, stating that instead of wheat starch 'chalk, lime, and particular marble bits, baked till it comes to a powder, is the method they use to sell it under the market price'. The cushion here is a pad around which hair would be built up; constructing this 'tete' was clearly a complicated operation.

Of a Tête de Mouton

This is intended in imitation of curls all over the head, and may be made in various forms, either upon a cawl or wires; which is a full dress for young ladies when any accident has happened to their hair; and some may have them made in a plainer manner, to wear in common with a cap; the fore-part to be in a smooth or rough toupee, according to fancy, and the back part to be in waves or promiscuous curls, which may be very useful for some ladies on account of warmth.
A Treatise on the Hair, **David Ritchie, 1770**

From the mid-1760s the fashion developed for tall headpieces, thirty centimetres above the head, and a decade later rising to over twice this amount. Marie Antoinette's coiffure was said to be over 90 centimetres tall. Such constructions might need the 'new invented Elastic Cushion', long pins, and a 'pole comb'; ladies wearing these would have to sleep sitting up. Such hair arrangements, involving hours of work, would be expected to last a number of weeks. At night nets would be worn over the hair to stop mice getting in – if they did there would be sufficient lard (to hold the powder in place) to keep them fairly well fed. *The Toilet of Flora* helpfully supplied recipes for destroying vermin and nits in hair.

A neck-braid

Ladies who have a great many short hairs falling from their braids on their shoulders, should have a neck braid under the hair, tied at the top; this braid's strings should be of ferret, and the hair should be parted where the neck strings goes, that it might not be seen.
TheArt of Hair-dressing, and Making it Grow Fast, William Moore, 1750

'Ferret' was, fortunately, a kind of silk.

The use of a cushion

A head of hair that is very thin and short may be made to appear very long, by having longer hair sewed in the cushion, which may be frizzed in with your own hair, when dressed, and if the hair is not long enough for curls, you may fasten a pair at the sides of the cushion, and frize a little of your own hair where the curls should be taken from, onto the false ones, which will make them look very natural.
The Art of Hair-dressing, and Making it Grow Fast, William Moore, 1750

'Frizzing' was curling the hair, while a cushion was a pad which the hair was combed over to make it look bigger. Hair could also be built up over a 'commode' described as 'a frame of wire, two or three stories high, fitted for the head'.

Men as well as women followed these fashions. From 1764 the men were often known as Macaronis, a reference to the Italian leg of the European grand tour, the essential finish for a young gentleman's social education.

To make powders of various colours

Take a pound of ivory black, in powder, and pass it through a sieve, and a pound of fine powder, which you must put on the fire, in a new saucepan, till it turns very black; then wet it with half an ounce of eau de Mareschalle. After that take of cloves, four drachms; cinnamon, two drachms; ginger, four drachms; dry these three pieces on a red-hot shovel; after that peel them, and beat them to a powder, so that they might pass through a sieve; then mix all together and the black powder will be done. This is the powder that is called the Poudre a la Mareschalle, and that serves to make up all the other kind of coloured powders, except the fair, the rose, and the red. It may be remarked that Mareschalle cannot be made properly in this country; all made here having a foetid, hot, disagreeable smell, and hurtful to the hair; while that from Paris is cool, sweet, wholesome and fragrant.

Palacocosmos, or the Whole Art of Hairdressing, 1782

From this it can be seen that wigs and hair were powdered not only in white. The application of eau de Mareshalle, an expensive perfume that by 1782 had been in use for ninety years, would seem to indicate that there was no status distinction between the different colours. Peeling such tiny amounts of the specified spices would be a tricky job, but necessary to ensure a fine powder.

Madame Rachel's secret ingredient

*In the interior of Sahara, or the Great Desert, is a
magnetic rock, from which a water distils, sparingly, in
the form of dew, which is possessed of extraordinary
properties. Whether a latent electricity be imparted by
the magnetism, or an additional quantity of oxygen
enters into its composition, it is not easy to say. But
it appears to have the property of increasing the
vital energies, as it restores the colour of grey hair,
apparently by renewing the circulation in its capillary*

FIRST INTRODUCTION   UNDER

tubes, the cessation of which occasions greyness; and it gives the appearance of youth to persons of considerable antiquity.
Beautiful For Ever, Madame Rachel, 1863

Madame Rachel, who claimed to have arranged 'the elegant cabinet toilet to the Sultana', and to have been 'especially appointed by the Princess Eugenie and the Court of France as sole importer of Arabian perfumes and toilette requisites', was quoting from the *Illustrated London News* of 24 January 1846; she

THE PLEASING RESULT.

claimed to have 'at an enormous expense, completed the purchase and sole right of the magnetic Rock Dew Water of Sahara' which 'gives the appearance of youth to persons far advanced in years, and removes wrinkles, defects and blemishes, from whatever cause they may arise ...'

Alas, Madame Rachel (real name Sarah Rachel Russell or Leverson) was not what she claimed, but this did not stop large numbers of extremely wealthy female clients passing over to her their jewels, thus preventing their husbands from finding out that they had paid hundreds of pounds for fairly simple treatments. It was this method of payment that led to Madame Rachel being tried for fraud and blackmail several times during the 1860s and 1870s. But wealthy and gullible clients could not resist her 'beautiful for ever' slogan, nor the promise offered by her 'face enameling' treatment, and she became extremely wealthy despite being unable to read or write.

In 1878 she was sentenced to five years in prison for fraud, with the judge, Sir John Huddleston, accusing her of following 'a calling which is about as detestable a one as I know of, for you have lived by pandering on the foibles and feeding upon the vanity of your fellow creatures of the same sex as yourself'. The *Illustrated Police News* on 9 March of that year vilified her as a greedy pantomime Jew. An article in the *Derby Mercury* responded on 17 April that 'Vanity has been a vice of women in all ages. Vice is too strong a term for it; indeed in some cases it might be called a virtue, for a woman without a little vanity is scarcely womanly'; encouraged by their husbands and brothers they 'begin to "get up" their faces a little … [and] buy all sorts of rubbish in the way of cosmetics'. So were not men partially to blame? Had not Madame Rachel assisted ladies in the age-old quest for desirability, with the cost of her treatments being the consumers' proof of their efficacy?

Madame Rachel died in prison two years later, aged 60.

A PAIR OF SPARKLING EYES

Though eyeshadow is a relatively modern introduction, eyeliner has been in use for millennia. Through the centuries different aspects of the eye have been the focus for cosmetic treatments: there are suggestions that a kind of kohl was used in the later medieval period, but little evidence for this is seen in paintings; the carpenter's wife in Chaucer's *Miller's Tale* plucks and possibly dyes her eyebrows but no mention is made of eyeshadow.

Renaissance ladies took belladonna to increase the size of their pupils, while in the late seventeenth and eighteenth centuries the shape of eyebrows was of major importance. We see a reference to a mascara-type product in *The Toilet of Flora* (1772), where various natural items are burnt to produce carbon to brush onto the eyelashes – lampblack was still being used in the nineteenth century, but also soot and burnt oak galls. By the early nineteenth century the idea of blue eyeshadow was still foreign, being noted as in use by Japanese ladies, according to *The Ladies Toilette*, (August 1806). Ten years later Lord Byron fell in love with an Italian woman 'not two and twenty – with great black Eastern eyes – and a vareity of subsidiary charms'; large eyes, associated with eastern beauty, remained a standard attraction throughout the century.

Eye colour

All colours do not equally grace the eyes; they are Cupid's torches, that should shine with a splendent flame, and never burn too blue; which is a colour looked upon as fatal. They are Cupid's crystal quivers, and must not be too big for that little archer, nor yet so small as not to contain his magazine of shafts. Those that have eyes of an ill colour, if they would have them black let them take:

Antimony washed and dried five ounces, lapis lazuli one ounce, musk, camfre, of each three grains, wood of aloes two ounces, frankincense three ounces, saffron half an ounce; make a very fine powder of all of these, at night when you go to bed put a little of it into the eyes, in the morning they will be as black as if they had been so naturally.

Artificial Embellishments, Thomas Jeamson, 1665

If your eyes are blood-shot, to remove that unseemly grievance

---

Take two ounces of the roots of red fennel, stamp them and press out the juice, and mingle it with half an ounce of clarified honey; heat them gently over the fire till they become an ointment, anoint therewith the eye-lids, and drop a drop with a feather into each eye; and in so doing, and in washing them with white wine or eyebright-water, the redness will vanish.

A rotten apple, bole-armeniac and bread, made into a poultice, by braying them in a mortar, and laying them

over the eyes, wetted a little with eyebright-water, between two fine cloths, will do the same.
The Accomplished Ladies Rich Closet of Rarities, 1687

Perhaps they were bloodshot from the application of the previous recipe?

Sir Hans Sloane's Eye Salve

Take prepared tutty one ounce, prepared bloodstone two scruples, aloes in fine powder twelve grains; mix them well together in a marble mortar with as much viper's fat as is requisite to bring the whole to the consistence of a soft salve. It is to be applied with an hair pencil, the eyes winking or a little opened; it has cured many whose eyes were covered with opaque films and scabs left by preceding disorders of the eyes.
The Toilet of Flora, 1775

Tutty was zinc oxide, used as an astringent.

Water for the eyes

A most approved water for the eyes; take a new-laid egg and roast it hard, then cut the shell in the midst and take out the yolk and put some white copporice where the yolk was, then bind the egg together again, and let it lie till it begin to be a water; then take the white forth from both sides of the egg, and put the same into a glass of fair

running water, and so let it stand a while; then strain it
through a fair linen cloth, and therewith wash your eyes
morning and evening.
The Ladies Dictionary, 1694

'Copporice' was copperas, in this case a sulphate of zinc, used medicinally as an astringent.

Eye-shadow

In applying rouge to the cheeks, keep it well up on the
cheek-bones and under the eyes, in order to give them a
brilliant and sparkling appearance. To add to the effect,
a little may be placed under the eye-brows, taking care,
however, not to let any get on the eyelids, as in that case the
eyes would have the appearance of old age or sorrow. Also
put the faintest tinge on the chin to brighten and throw up
the complexion. Lastly, with a burnt amber pencil paint
a fine line under the lower eyelashes and "touch up" the
lashes themselves with black cosmetic. Many actresses use
an immense amount of blue grease-paint on the eye lids. It
throws up the eyes.
Myra's Journal, 1 August 1900

But note, this blue eyeshadow is only for actresses.

Green eye-shadow

Green make-up in the form of eyeshadow or powder should always be bought from a very reliable source, as arsenic is sometimes found in make-up of this colour.
The Way to Beauty; a complete guide to personal loveliness,
Sonya Jolsen, 1937

It is remarkable that toxic materials were being used in cosmetics as late as this.

APPLICATION OF EYE-SHADOW
(A) Method for small, deep-set eyes
(B) Method for large eyes

Eye-liner

The fashion of laying on a streak of some dark cosmetic along the edge of the eyelid is a very old Oriental custom, which has of late been practised, not altogether without success, in England. It has the effect of making the eyes appear larger and more brilliant than they actually are; but while the ancients used a preparation of sulphide of antimony, which they called kohol, the perfumers of our own day produce the same effect by the simple means of a little Indian ink and rose-water.
How to Preserve Good Looks, 1871

Removing dried Indian ink from the eyelids cannot have been fun.

Long lashes

Long eyelashes are seldom preserved in this country after thirty years of age, because their growth is neglected. If examined through a magnifying glass, when the eyelashes begin to decline, the extremities will be found split. If these extremities are clipped with scissors every six weeks, not only will the eyelashes be preserved, but they will increase in strength, and assume the curve so becoming to a beautiful pair of women's eyes. By this practice, long eyelashes may be obtained, even at an advanced period of life.
The Handbook of the Toilette, 1839

In 1964 there was a curious fashion for extending the eyelashes by sticking individual false lashes to the existing hairs, with the additions being human hair, or hairs of mink or sable.

Scanty eyelashes

Eyelashes, if too scanty or thin, may be strengthened and stimulated into growth by a gentle massage of the edges of the eyelids, using a little olive oil.

Avoid the use of 'eyelash growers' containing cantharides, as the same may injure the eye if any of the preparation should get into it. Using the eyebrow brush for the eyelashes, by brushing them upward from the underside, will encourage their growth and will give them an attractive little upward curl.

The Beauty Book, Roxana Rion, 1913

Cantharides (also known as Spanish Fly) raises blisters, makes the skin red, and is supposedly an aphrodisiac.

Eyelash dyeing

The eyelashes seldom require dyeing; when they do, the colouring matter should be carefully applied by another person. The eye should be closed, a bit of flattened wood placed under the lashes and these coloured with a fine black-lead pencil. If a permanent dye be required, it must be used carefully. The eyelashes must be placed upon the bit of wood

as before, and each carefully touched with a strong aqueous
solution of carbonate of soda, applied by means of a fine
camel-hair pencil. The moment the eyelashes are dry, a little
marking ink for linen should be put carefully on. In this
operation, very little liquid must be taken in the camel-hair
pencil, and very great caution observed, lest either the soda
or the ink touch the skin at the root of the eyelash, and dye
it black, or perhaps produce inflammation.
The Handbook of the Toilette, 1839

Good eyelashes

Good eyelashes go a long way towards establishing a
claim to beauty for the eyes. They should be long, glossy
and curling outwards from the cheek. Chloride of gold
dyes the lashes and eyebrows a very satisfactory brown,
also whiskers. When the growth of the lashes has been
interrupted or destroyed by the action of fire, the following
will be found to be beneficial. Five grains of sulphate of
quinine to an ounce of sweet almond oil. Apply to the roots
of the lashes with the finest sable pencil. This must be very
gently and carefully applied. It is almost impossible to
perform this delicate office for one's self.
Sylvia's Book of the Toilet, 1881

Brows of the eyes, how to beautify and adorn

Brows of the glittering eyes are Cupid's groves of
pleasure, where he shelters himself from the violent heat

of the two flaming opticks, or rather as a controlling intelligence, made superintendent to the crystal spheres below him; he keeps his residence there, that he might with the more facility direct their beamy influences when and whither he please. You ladies may by this means make them beautiful.

Brows that have their hair growing too thick or irregular:

Take ivy, gum, newts' eggs, or pincent colophonie [a resin made by distilling water and turpentine], leeches burnt, half an ounce; grind and mingle them with the blood of a frog, and anoint the superfluous hair and it will come off.

Or you may take the juice of henbane, dragons blood, gum Arabic and frankincense, of each three drams, juice of nightshade as much as will suffice it to make into an ointment, and apply it as the former.

A Ladies Dictionary, 1694

The introductory text here is lifted from Thomas Jeamson's *Artificial Embellishments* (1665); but Jeamson's original text suggests using a pair of tweezers instead of these rather dodgy recipes.

Two recipes to 'change the eyebrows black'

Rub them frequently with ripe elderberries. Some use burnt cork, or cloves burnt in the candle; others prefer the black of frankincense, rosin, and mastic. This black will not melt or come off through the person's sweat.

First wash your eyebrows with a decoction of gall

nuts; then wet them with a pencil or little brush dipped in
a solution of green vitriol, in which a little gum Arabic
has been dissolved, and when dry they will appear of a
beautiful black colour.
The Toilet of Flora, 1775

An ointment for lice in the eybrows

Take one apple roasted and cleansed, quicksilver killed
[neutralised] with spittle, mix them well and anoint.
Cosmeticks, or the Beautifying Parts of Physick, Johann
Wecker, 1660

Headlice are never a good look, especially on the eyebrows.
Mercury neutralised with saliva is a curious ingredient,
though in fact the saliva may have helped the skin absorb
the mercury. Possibly the apple paste helped it to stick to
the hair, and kill the lice. It is to be hoped that this remedy
worked quickly.

How to redress beetle brows, or those that fall unseemly too low over the eyes

The juice of colewort leaves two ounces, mastic beaten
finely into powder half an ounce, spirit of sulphur two
drams, oil of turpentine three drams, incorporate these by
a gentle simmering over a fire, and dipping a little brush
in the composition, go often over a strong forehead cloth
with it, till it is very wet, then going to bed, place it over

the eyebrows, binding it on hard and straight upwards,
that it may draw up the eye-brows as high as the skin will
permit, and when you take it off, wash the forehead-cloth
and eye-brows with water, wherein allom [alum] has been
dissolved, and renew [this on] the forehead every evening
for a week, and the eye-brows, by the contracting of the
skin that before was too loose, will fix in their proper place,
so that the party will seem so altered, especially upon a first
view, as scarcely to be known for the same man or woman.
Beauties Treasury, 1705

In the eighteenth century eyebrows were plucked to make them high and round, sometimes leading to a need for replacements.

A mono-brow

When the eyebrows meet in the middle line, and
consequently give a severe and often unpleasant expression
to the face, their prominence is removed by decolorising
the centre with peroxide of hydrogen, which renders the
hairs at the root of the nose where the eyebrows meet less
conspicuous.

    If this does not produce a sufficient effect, the eyebrows
are soaped over so that the hairs lie smoothly, and all
offending hairs are then gently rubbed off with the pointed
end of a piece of pumice stone.
The Secrets of Beauty, Cora Brown Potter, 1914

Of the Eye-Brow

Each eye-brow should form an arch upon the forehead, the hollow of which makes a small vault above the eye. The head of the eye-brow should be thicker than the tail; the intercil, or space between the eye-brows, quite free of hair.

If the eye-brows are too thick, all the help that is to be made is very carefully to clip off some of the tops of the hairs, an operation so nice that the persons must not venture to do it themselves, as it will only make them grow thicker. An application of the oil of nuts is very serviceable in this case; or the eye-brows may be frequently rubbed with a lye made of the ashes of burnt cabbage.
The Art of Preserving Beauty, 1789

It is not clear why doing this job yourself would make the hairs grow thicker, but not if someone else performs the operation. The writer of this text provides over four pages of advice on the eyebrows, without once mentioning mice, but including instructions on how to deal with hair loss

from the eyebrows, relocating them (using a razor and unguents), dyeing, plucking, and rectifying the defect of an eyebrow 'too much elevated', which was to be 'in some degree palliated by assuming a modest, downcast look, which attention will soon render habitual'.

Mouse-skin eyebrows

Mrs Clerimont: ... Oh bless me Jenny, I am so plane, I am afraid of myself – I have not laid on half red enough – what a dogh-baked thing I was before I improved myself, and travelled for beauty – however, my face is very prettily designed today.

Fainlove: Indeed, madam you begin to have so fine an hand, that you are younger every day than other.

Mrs Clerimont: The Ladies abroad used to call me Mrs Titian, I was so famous for my colouring; but prethee, Wench, bring me my black eye-brows out of the next room.

Jenny: Madam, I have them in my hand.

Fainlove: It would be happy for all that are to see you today, if you could change your eyes too.

Mrs Clerimont: Gallant enough – no hang it, I'll wear these I have on ...

The Tender Husband (Act 3), Richard Steele, c. 1707

High arching eyebrows were deemed essential in the early eighteenth century. When a lady's eyebrows did not match the required shape they were shaved off and replaced by false eyebrows — a lady might have a selection to choose from. It has been supposed that these were made from mouse-skin, with the hair retained, but there is no simple evidence for this. Jonathan Swift's poem 'A Beautiful Young Nymph Going to Bed' (1734) contains the famous lines:

Her eyebrows from a mouse's hide
Stuck on with art on either side,
Pulls off with care, and first displays 'em,
Then in a play-book smoothly lays 'em.

This is supported by another satirical poem printed in the *London Daily Post* on 19 June 1736, containing the lines:

Or Nightly Traps insidious lay,
To catch new Eye-brows for the Day.

Corinna, Swift's 'nymph', evidently takes great care of her false eyebrows, which are protected from attack during the night by vermin, unlike her plaster and hairpiece. The poem does not spare Corinna at all — she has a 'crystal eye', false teeth, a wig infested with fleas, 'flabby dugs' and plumpers — lumps of cork kept in the mouth to fill out the cheeks after rotten teeth had been removed. And for those readers with a very strong constitution, Swift's *The Lady's Dressing Room* (1732) shows the reality of the body behind:

the gallypots and vials placed,
Some filled with washes, some with paste,
Some with pomatum, paints and slops,
And ointments

No doubt most of this reflected reality; but with regards to false eyebrows made of mouse-skin, actual evidence of how to prepare your mouse is hard to find.

DESIRABLE LIPS AND
SWEET BREATH

The desirability of red lips is mentioned in early medieval texts in the British Isles, though specific recipes do not appear until much later. But obviously and provocatively reddened lips have throughout history provoked debates about the morality of cosmetics. Dr Doris M Odlum of Bournemouth was quoted in the *Western Morning News* on 31 January 1936 as saying 'Although I must admit I have never been terribly keen on lip-stick myself, still, if it gives some people satisfaction to use it, I do not regard it as a sign of moral depravity.'

Red pomatum for the lips

Take an ounce of white wax and of an ox's marrow, three ounces of white pomatum, and melt all in a bath-heat. Add a dram of alkanet, and stir the mass together till it acquires a red colour.

Others choose to use the ointment of roses, which is thus prepared:

Take hog's lard washed in rose-water, red roses, and pale roses; beat all in a mortar, mix them together, and let them macerate for two days. Then melt the lard and strain it, and

add the same quantity of roses as before. Let them macerate
in the fat for two days, and afterwards let the mass boil in a
bath-heat. Strain it with expression, and keep it for use.

Some are accustomed to wash their lips with pure
brandy, in order to make them look red.
Abdeker: or, the Art of Preserving Beauty, 1756

The writer of *The Toilet of Flora* (1775) offered a much
more pleasant-sounding recipe involving fresh butter,
beeswax and grapes, rather than lard. But the use of rose
petals perhaps redeems this one. The plant alkanet has for
millennia been used as a source of red dye; the roots are
crushed to produce the colour.

Lip salve, or pomatum for the lips

Take half a pound of caul of mutton cut into pieces, and
melt it in a little saucepan, and pass it through a piece
of cloth, and put in another pan four ounces of wax, and
when melted mix it with the mutton grease; then put in
balm of oil mixed together, and melt it in the balneum
mariae; when it is almost cold, pour in it four drachms of
carmine, and stir it till the pomatum be of a rose colour;
and then grind it well upon marble, and melt it again in
the balneum mariae; when it is melted and cold, put some
essence of rose in, and the pomatum or salve is done.
Palacocosmos, or the Whole Art of Hairdressing, 1782

The caul is the fatty membrane surrounding the intestines
of a mammal, which as a coating for the lips would

both nourish and protect, though it might not appeal to modern sensibilities.

Lip loveliness

So many women make up their lips badly. Either they wear too much or too little lipstick, or they look as if they had tried to apply it while on a bus or somewhere equally unsuitable. I have actually seen women rummage surreptitiously in their handbag, produce a lipstick, and with a hasty glance round to see that they are unobserved, rub the lipstick over their mouth with guilty abandon and return it to their bag with a satisfied smirk on their faces. Needless to say, the major part of the lip-rouge has not gone on to the lips at all, but is smeared around the surrounding skin in the most alarming fashion.
The Way to Beauty, Jane Clare, 1938

The scientific breakthrough that created lip salve as a solid stick was achieved only towards the end of the nineteenth century, with the word 'lipstick' being recorded from 1880. Jane Clare gives much useful advice on the applying of lipstick. Elsewhere in her book she writes:

It is possible to improve the shape of a mouth enormously by using a good thick, indelible lipstick, and if necessary going over the edge of the actual lip in order to deepen its curve. But I do not advise you to do this unless you are very expert, because if it is badly done it can look quite dreadful, and it smudges very easily.

Note — An over-pronounced cupid's bow gives a prim, mimsy look, and to extend the curve of the upper lip outwards can easily make you look as if you had a bad smell under your nose! So take warning.

To make the lips ruddy

Paleness, when once it affects the lips, makes the world believe that those ruby portals of the mouth have lost their varnish by being too much knocked at. Those ladies whose lips lie under such a suspicion may beautify them with a coral complexion thus.

Take the shavings of your deepest coloured brazil, three ounces; make them into a very fine powder, steep it three days in three pints of fair spring water, then add six drams of fish glue bruised and minced; let it stand till it becomes soft and dissolves, then set it over the fire again and add grana tinctoria (chermes berries) four ounces, rock alum one ounce, borax three drams; boil all these till half be consumed, strain it and in a glass vessel keep it close stopped eight days before you use it. It gives a very amiable redness to pale or blue parts, whether lips or cheeks; that which you put on at one time will last eight days, in which time it will not be done off either by sweat or water.
Artificial Embellishments, Thomas Jeamson, 1665

'Brazil' was the name given to the sappan, a tree native to the East Indies, which gave a strong and valuable red dye. After the European discovery of America the name was extended and gradually transferred to a different tree found in an area which came to be known as 'terra de Brasil', eventually shortened to Brazil. Chermes berries were indeed thought to be berries, but were in fact the dried bodies of insects (specifically the pregnant female of *Coccus ilicis*) which, like cochineal, gives a strong red dye.

The smell from the fish glue must have been interesting, especially after eight days.

Lip-salve

A quarter of a pound of hard marrow, from the marrow bone. Melt it over a slow fire; as it dissolves gradually, pour the liquid marrow into an earthen pipkin [bottle], then add to it an ounce of spermaceti, twenty raisins of the sun, stoned, and a small portion of alkanna root, sufficient to colour it a bright vermilion. Simmer these ingredients over a slow fire for ten minutes, then strain the whole through muslin; and while hot, stir into it one tea-spoonful of the balsam of Peru. Pour it into the boxes in which it is to remain; it will there stiffen, and become fit for use.
Mirror of the Graces, 1811

'Alkanna' here is alkanet. There may be an indication here of the mixture being poured into a mould, so that it can be used as a solid like a modern lipstick; whether it would be applied directly or with a brush would depend on how much it stiffened. Possibly the degree of stiffening required would be only sufficient to stop it melting from the warmth of the lips. 'Raisins of the sun' were sun-dried grapes.

How to smooth the lips when they are rough and chapped

*When those pretty sister rubies have been kissed too hard,
either by a chilly and cold-mouthed Boreas [north wind],
or a scorching and hot-lipped Sol [sun], to repair the
breaches such rude embraces make on their cherry skins,
use these things following, Ladies, they will make them
seem such smooth and blushing wax as Cupid will think
himself honoured to imprint his kisses on.*

*Take stag's suet two pounds, fresh lard six ounces, wash
them often in white wine, then work them well together
till all the white wine be pressed out. Then put it into an
earthenware glazed vessel, adding nardus indicus [Indian
spikenard] three grains, cloves half an ounce, nutmegs two
drams, seven or eight pippins [apples] pared, cored and
sliced; steep all these one whole day in sufficient quantity
of rosewater, then keeping it covered, set it over a gentle
fire, stirring it up and down with a wooden spatula till all
the rose-water be evaporated. Strain it through a thick cloth
into a clean vessel half full of rose-water; let it stand till
the suet be cold and swims on the top of the water, then put
it again into an earthenware pot, adding oil of almonds six
ounces, virgins' wax four ounces; melt all these over the fire,
strain it again into rose-water through a thick cloth, let it
as before stand till it is cold, then take that off which swims
on the top of the rose-water and wash it well in some scented
water till it be white as snow; then keep it for your use in a
dry place, so that it do not mould. Some add to this pomatum
coral finely powdered to make it the more drying. Others
add juice of alkanet to give it a vermilion colour.*

There is nothing better than this for any chaps whatever.
Artificial Embellishments, Thomas Jeamson, 1665

A time-traveller from the seventeenth century visiting a modern cosmetics counter would surely look at the lipstick display in wonder, and ask how we spend the vast leisure time available to us. If all this seems too much, Jeamson offers a simpler alternative:

Take a fine linen rag, dip it in the juice of houseleek, and apply it to the lips.

Or even:

Michael Nostradame, a Frenchman, much commends cotton dipped in common oil and laid to the navel going to bed. It is an easy thing and soon tried.

Nostradamus' remedy should perhaps be taken with a pinch of salt.

A dentifrice

Fine powder of pumice stone . . . . 4 parts
*   Ditto of cuttle fish bone . . . . 4 parts*
*   Ditto of prepared chalk . . . . 4 parts*
*   Add a sprinkling of sub-carbonate of soda, mix them well together, colour and scent according to the taste, and then pass it through a fine sieve.*

*   In this mixture it will be found that the hard pumice stone abrades, the cuttle-fish bone produces a polish, the chalk will absorb and the soda neutralise the acid. In cases*

where the enamel is decomposing, where the green or brown exists, this mixture is to be used, and with a hard brush. This same powder will also be found useful for the dotted, or honey-combed teeth, and will polish the surface and remove the dark spots.
Beauty's Mirror, 1839

'Honey-combed teeth' sound beyond salvation.

A powder to whiten the teeth

Take of ginger, cinnamon, cloves, pumice-stone, wood of aloes, nutmeg, mace, each half an ounce; pepper, pellitory of Spain, mustard-seed, stavesacre, each three ounces; sponge, white marble, of each half an ounce; date-stones burnt, white hellebore, of each two ounces; barley bread burnt with salt and honey, half an ounce; red tiles, burnt harts-horn, feathered alum, olive-stones burnt, myrobalan-stones burnt, each three ounces. Mix them and make a fine powder.
Cosmeticks, or the Beautifying Parts of Physick, Johann Wecker, 1660

This is quite a shopping list. Pellitory of Spain, also called Spanish camomile, was formerly used against toothache; and stavesacre is a plant formerly used against vermin. The various abrasives – pumice, marble, tiles and the fruit stones – would have cleaned deposits off the teeth, but ultimately would have attacked the enamel too.

A coral stick for the teeth

*Make a stiff paste with tooth powder and a sufficient
quantity of mucilage of gum tragacanth; form with this
paste little cylindrical rollers, the thickness of a large
goose quill, about three inches in length. Dry them in the
shade. The method of using these corals is to rub them
against the teeth, and in proportion as they waste, the teeth
get cleaner; they serve instead of tooth powders, opiates or
prepared roots, but they are brittle and apt to break, and on
this account are less convenient than tooth powder that is
used with the prepared roots.*
The Toilet of Flora, 1775

To sweeten the breath

*At night going to bed, chew about the quantity of a small
nut of fine myrrh. Or chew every night and morning a
clove, a piece of Florentine orrice-root about the size of
a small bean, or the same quantity of burnt alum.*
The Toilet of Flora, 1775

The *Romaunt de la Rose* of the fourteenth century describes
the use of mint and myrrh as a mouthwash. Given the
standard English diet of ale, meat and bread, with sugar
as often as you could get it, bad breath must have been
fairly standard.

Sweet scented troches to correct a bad breath

Take frankincense a scruple, ambergris fifteen grains,
musk seven grains, oil of lemons six drops, double refined
sugar an ounce, and form into little troches with mucilage
of gum Arabic, made with cinnamon water. Hold one or
two in the mouth as often as occasion requires.
The Toilet of Flora, 1775

Troches were lozenges. The quantity of sugar would have helped rot the teeth.

Mouthwash

The mouth should be rinsed, and the throat gargled with
tepid water, to which a few drops of Eau de Cologne
may be added with advantage, every morning; for a kind
of mucus gathers upon the surface of the mouth, and
particularly on the tongue, during the hours of sleep.
    If the mouth feels clammy during the day, one part
of port wine mingled with three parts of water forms a
refreshing lotion to rinse it with.
Toilet Table Talk, 1856

To make the teeth white

Take one drop of oil of vitriol, and wet the teeth with it, and then rub them afterwards with a coarse cloth; and though the medicine be strange, fear it not.
The Ladies Delight, Hannah Woolley, 1672

On the contrary, be very afraid; oil of vitriol is concentrated sulphuric acid.

LOVELY HANDS AND
GORGEOUS NAILS

Deirdre, the heroine of the early medieval *Book of Leinster*, refers to colouring her fingernails, but it was not until the twentieth century that nail varnish provided a permanent hard coating for nails; nail varnish seems to have been inspired by car paint. But early on women shaped and stained their fingernails — even Anglo-Saxon nuns were criticised for tending their fingernails and their hair curls.

Nails, to remedy the vices incident to them

Nails of the hands are pearly helmets wherewith prudent nature hath armed the active fingers, to which if they be neatly burnished, they give a commanding comeliness, and may at a pressing exigency be fit materials to head Cupid's penetrating shafts. Pare your nails smooth and decently, but not with so much overstrictness that you cut them too near your fingers, cause them to be sore, and so instead of seemly render them unseemly; if they grow muddy or cloudy on the superfices you may gently scrape them with a piece of fine glass, and they will flourish and be the more lively.
The Ladies Dictionary, 1694

Nail care

Some women find that intense heat or intense cold renders their finger-nails brittle. This condition may often be cured or obviated by rubbing almond oil thoroughly into them at night. Nails of this character should be cut with sharp scissors, not filed, and they ought always to be soaked in hot water beforehand, but should never be exposed to great fire-heat in an ungloved state.

I have occasionally been called upon to decide what seems rather a knotty point to some women: Ought the nails to be cut square or rounded? In my opinion there is only one reply to this question. It is this: Don't cut them at all, but file them off according to the shape of your finger-tips.
Beauty Culture, H Ellen Browning, 1898

For pilled [peeled] nails

Take of salt, flour of barley, costmary powdered, each one part, honey a sufficient quantity; mix them.
Cosmeticks, or the Beautifying Parts of Physick, Johann Wecker, 1660

Pilled, or peeled, nails were thin nails; salt and honey would have helped protect against infection, and the costmary (*Balsamita vulgaris*) would have been antiseptic and anti-inflammatory. All in all this treatment would have strengthened the nails.

Nail tinting

A pomade which is simply for tinting the nails is this:
> *Nail rouge*
> *Powdered carmine (fine) . . . . 1 drachm*
> *Fresh lard . . . . 2 drachms*
> *Oil of bergamot. . . . . 24 drops*
> *Essence of Cyprus . . . . 12 drops*
> *Beat all the ingredients together in a mortar and heat in a bain-marie, stirring as before to a smooth paste. Apply to the nails with a camel's hair brush or bit of absorbent cotton, and after a few minutes wipe off with fine linen.*
> **The Woman Beautiful, Ella Adelia Fletcher, 1899**

Liquid nail polish, as opposed to varnish, was widely used in the first decades of the twentieth century. The *Daily Mail* on 26 February 1929 reported that the Queen had bought nail polish in Woolworths in Bognor.

Beauty Aids Women Are Buying

A new nail varnish has captured attention for the moment. It has a peculiar finish, when dry, of pink mother-of-pearl, and is used by those who like something out of the common.
Daily Mail, **3 September 1928**

Michelle Menard, who worked for the cosmetics company Revlon, is generally credited with the invention of nail varnish in the 1920s.

Nail varnishes

Non-transparent varnishes can be bought in almost any colour. It is not necessary to use a dark shade in order to cover the quick-line. Dark varnishes should only be used on a perfectly groomed hand belonging to a beautifully dressed woman. Nothing looks more vulgar and shoddy than violent-coloured badly cared-for nails worn with unsuitable clothes. Generally speaking, they should be confined to town-ensembles. The softer shades are much better taste with country clothes.

The Way to Beauty, Jane Clare, 1938

Manicure

Careless cutting of the nails is to be avoided; and as for that relic of barbarism, 'biting' nails – pardon me, the subject is too unpleasant even to think of. Avoid excesses in manicuring, such as fancy shaped nails or extra polished. Remember that the secret of good manicuring is not to attract attention to the nails, but rather to avoid the attention usually given nails either too little or too much manicured.

The Beauty Book, Roxana Rion, 1913

Hands, how to beautify them

Hands that are fair and beautiful are highly admired and esteemed; they are, Ladies, the fleshy altars where your supposititious inamoratos offer to you as female deities the first fruits of their devotion in zealous kisses. Hands in the first place that are chapped, as sometimes the most curious [careful] will, must in the morning be rubbed over with your own spittle, then anoint them with duck or capon's grease, well washed in rose-water.
The Ladies Dictionary, 1694

See page 56, the use of spittle as a treatment for crow's feet.

Clean hands

To make a water that taketh off all staining, dyeing and spots from the hands of artificers, that get them by working, and maketh them very white and fair. It is also good for them that be sunburned.

Take the juice of a lemon with a little bay salt, and wash your hands with it, and let them dry of themselves. Wash them again, and you shall find all the spots and stainings gone. It is also very good against the scurf or scabs.
The Treasury of Commodious Conceites and Hidden Secrets, John Partridge, 1584

An excellent hand-water, or washing water, very cheap

Take a gallon of fair water, one handful of lavender-flowers, a few cloves, and some oris-powder, and four ounces of benjamin; distil the water in an ordinary leaden still. You may distil a second water by a new infusion of water upon the lees; a little of this will sweeten a basin of fair water for your table.
Delightes for Ladies to Adorn their Persons, 1636

An indication that seventeenth-century ladies would be required to have basic lab skills, while the use of 'fair' water shows that people were aware of different degrees of quality of water. 'Oris-powder' was powdered orris root.

Night gloves

To wash and prepare night gloves to keep the hands white, smooth and soft.

Take pure white wax four pound, Spermacetis two ounces, oil of the greater cold seeds cleansed and drawn without fire, and Magistery of Bismuth or Tinglass of each three drams, Borax and burnt Allum finely powdered of each half a dram, put them all into a Pipkin [bottle], which set in a Kettle of hot boiling water, and when they are melted, stir them well together, to incorporate them. Then having washed first your gloves in several waters and steeped them twelve hours in cream, dip them in this composition whilst it is hot.

The said Composition is good also to dip cloths in and spread them for to line womens masks, it preserves the Complexion of Ladies. The Ladies in France use it for both. It is also a good Cosmetic, anointing the face with it at night going to bed, washing it oft in the morning with some Cosmetick water.

The True Preserver and Restorer of Health, George Hartman, 1682

Gloves were often made of dog skin, though confusingly this term was also used for a kind of sheepskin. Night gloves were still being used in the Victorian period, when soft, white hands were considered highly desirable. The 'magistery' of a mineral was a term from alchemy, signifying that part which carried the material's potency; here it probably means a purified concentrate.

THE BODY BEAUTIFUL

Make-up and beauty treatments apply to all parts of the body, of course; not just the face and hair. Body shape has been the subject of recipes and regimes for thousands of years, while for a Victorian gentleman the whiteness of a lady's hand was all-important.

In 1652 Agrippa von Nettesheim's *The Glory of Women* urged the viewer of a beautiful woman to 'take view of her round and dimpled Chinne, in a pleasant manner, under which the neck is placed, which is small, but something long, fairly erected upon her round shoulders, a delicate throat, white, and of an indifferent thicknesse, her voice sweet and pleasant, her breast somewhat large and prominent, adorned with two *nectar*-fill'd Paps, the roundnesse of which, doth suite and agree well with the roundnesse of her belly, her sides soft, back smooth, and erect, armes stretched out, hands small and slender, fingers fitly jointed, her flanks and hips more full, the calves of her legs more fleshy, the tips of her hands and feet ending in a round orbicular completeness, and every member full of juice and moisture.' One wonders how Agrippa himself would have fared if subjected to a similar checklist.

To put on weight evenly

*If one part fall away and bear no proportion to the rest of
the body you may bring it to even terms thus: take oil of
foxes an ounce and a half, oil of lilies, the grease of capons
and geese, of each two ounces, Greek pitch, pine rosin, and
turpentine, of each two ounces; boil all these together in an
earthernware glazed vessel, adding oil of elder one ounce;
then take it from the fire and add new wax, as much as will
suffice to make it into a fine stiff cerecloth [bandage]; when
it is almost cold spread it upon a strong cloth, as much as will
wrap up the member; then apply it and leave it on all night.*
Artificial Embellishments, Thomas Jeamson, 1665

'Oil of foxes' was produced by skinning and deboning a
fox, and boiling the flesh with oil and herbs; the liquid
was strained and kept for use usually as a liniment for
muscular pain. Presumably it was believed that it would
build up the strength of a weakened limb.

Weight control, Venetian style

*Among the Venetians, the maids, when they are to be
coupled in marriage, they are kept very daintily, to the end
they may become more fat, well-liking, & in good plight,
they use dished wheat with milk, they sleep longer in the
daytime, they live very idly close cooped up, that at length
they may grow fat as crammed capons; therefore they
feed upon unctuous and sweet meats, that they may more
daintily, and with a more trim grace be dedicated to their*

bridegroom. This artifice is used to accommodate the fancy
of the men of that nation; for the Italians desire to have
their women thick, well set, and plump.
Man Transform'd: or the Artificial Changeling, John Bulwer, 1653

Bulwer castigates women less for putting on weight
than for using corsets to pretend to lose it. 'Cramming
capons' was a way of force-feeding chickens to make them
excessively weighty.

To make the body or any part thereof plump and fat, that was before too lean

Take twelve or thirteen lizards or newts, cut off their heads
and tails, boil them and let the water stand to cool; take off
the grease, mix it with wheat flour, feed a hen therewith
till she be fat, then kill her and eat her; this often used will
make you exceeding fat. Keep it for a rare and true secret.
Artificial Embellishments, Thomas Jeamson, 1665

Straight-lacing

Another foolish affectation there is in young virgins, though
grown big enough to be wiser, but that they are led blindfold
by custom to a fashion pernicious beyond imagination; who
thinking a slender waist a great beauty, strive all that they
possibly can by straight-lacing themselves to attain unto a
wand-like smallness of waist, never thinking themselves
fine enough until they can span their waist.

By which deadly artifice they reduce their breasts into
such straights that they soon purchase stinking breath; and
while they ignorantly affect an angust or narrow breast,
and to that end by strong compulsion shut up their waists
in a whale-bone prison, or little-ease; they open a door to
consumptions, and a withering rottenness.
Man Transform'd: or the Artificial Changeling, John Bulwer, 1653

John Bulwer was a pioneering student of the nature of
human gesture and of the potential for communication
by deaf people. His study of the processes of artifical
modification of the human body uses examples from all
over the known world, and ultimately criticises British
fashions for using the same restricting actions applied by
less developed cultures. A 'whale-bone prison, or little-ease'
was a corset, made from the baleen plates from whales'
mouths. The *Illustrated Police News* of 25 June 1870
carried the story of a woman who 'died from the effects of
tight lacing which impeded the action of her heart'.

Perspiration

The chief enemy of personal daintiness is perspiration. If
you suffer even slightly from this problem take yourself in
hand here and now and eradicate the trouble either by using
one of the very excellent deodorants now on the market,
or you can make one for yourself out of a 4oz. tin of zinc
ointment with a 1/2oz. of zinc carbonate added to it. This
should be applied at night and washed off in the morning.
The Way to Beauty, Jane Clare, 1938

An ointment for to make the hair fall from any place of the body

Take the whites of three new-laid eggs well beaten; eight ounces of quicklime, an ounce of orpiment: beat it into powder; put so much among the eggs as may make it a thin paste, then with a pencil anoint the place which you intend to clear from hair, leaving it on for a quarter of an hour, or some time longer, then wash it with warm water, and the hair will fall off; you then anoint the place with oil of roses.
The Laboratory, or School of Arts, Godfrey Smith, 1738

The use of 'quicklime' should ring warning bells; calcium oxide can cause severe burns and in this case, mixed with arsenic trisulphide (orpiment), which is toxic, would certainly take off hair, and probably some of the skin underneath. Definitely not recommended. The use of the word 'pencil' to mean a brush lasted into the nineteenth century.

Superfluous hair

No matter how beautifully formed your limbs, if they have an ugly growth of hair on them their outline cannot fail to be marred, and the most lovely mouth in the world can be spoilt by a dark shadow at its corners. Underarm neatness is a tremendously important point to study. Untidiness at this point can completely ruin a smart ensemble. Incidentally, you may very easily find that the good old-fashioned razor is the best way of dealing

with hair on your underarm. Dust thickly with absorbent powder afterwards.
The Way to Beauty, Jane Clare, 1938

Remedies for the galling, fretting and sweating of the feet

The body, that fleshy palace of a deathless guest, would sink beneath its own magnificence, were it not upheld by the feet, those beauteous pedestals to the sister columns that more immediately support the structure. If they are once fretted, or stand on too moist a foundation, they may chance to slip, and so the whole edifice of beauty hazard itself by catching a fall. Your wisest way will be to secure them thus:

The feet, if they are often subject to troublesome sweatings may thus be ordered: bathe them in warm water wherein alum hath been dissolved; or else wash your feet in water [with] the flowers and berries of myrtle, the leaves of cypress, tamarisk, mint, marjoram. And after you have washed them well, anoint them with litharge powdered and mixed with honey.
Artificial Embellishments, Thomas Jeamson, 1665

A remedy for moist feet, etc

Be careful to keep the feet always washed clean, and frequently change your stockings and shoes. Take twenty pounds of a lye made of the ashes of the bay-tree, three

*handfuls of bay leaves, a handful of sweet flag, and the
same quantity of calamus aromaticus, and dittany of
Crete[a medicinal plant]; boil the whole together some time,
then strain off the liquor, and add two quarts of wine. Steep
your feet in this bath an hour every day, and in a short time
the feet will no longer exhale a disagreeable smell.*
The Toilet of Flora, 1775

An aromatic bath

*Boil, in a sufficient quantity of river water, one or more
of the following plants; viz. laurel, thyme, rosemary, wild
thyme, sweet-marjoram, bastard-marjoram, lavender,
southernwood, wormwood, sage, pennyroyal, sweet-basil,
balm, wild mint, hyssop, roses, pinks, clove-july-flowers,
wall-flowers, stocks, anise, fennel, or any other herbs that
have an agreeable scent. Having strained off the liquor
from the herbs, add thereto a little brandy or camphorated
spirits of wine.*

*This is an excellent bath to strengthen the limbs; it
removes aches and pains proceeding from cold, promotes
perspiration, and causes the body to exhale an agreeable
odour.*
The Toilet of Flora, 1775

A bath to mundify [cleanse] the body

*Take of pellitory of the wall, mallows, bears-breech,
violet leaves, each one handful; whole barley two pugils*

*[handfuls]; violet, chamomile flowers, each three pugils;
make a decoction in rain-water, and with that make a bath,
with which wash, fasting; afterwards when the body hath
sweated in the bed, wipe it carefully.*

*Or, to cleanse the body and make it comely, take of
sage, lavender-flowers, rose-flowers, each two handfuls, a
little salt, boil them in water or in a lye, and make a bath
not too hot, in which bathe the body two hours before meat.*
**Cosmeticks, or the Beautifying Parts of Physick, Johann
Wecker, 1660**

Bear-breech or bear's breech is acanthus, also known as
'brank ursine'; it was supposed to be good for gout and
cramp.

A sweet-scented bath for Noble-women

*Take of roses, citron pill, citron flowers, orange flowers,
jasmine, bay, rosemary, lavender, mint, pennyroyal,
spring-water, each a sufficient quantity; boil them together
and make a bath; to which add oil of spike (French
lavender) six drops, musk five grains, ambergris three
grains, sweet asa one ounce; let her go into the bath two
hours before meat.*
**Cosmeticks, or the Beautifying Parts of Physick, Johann
Wecker, 1660**

Citron pill was the rind, not the seed. Asa was asafoetida,
a fragrant gum. Musk and ambergris would have been
available only to the wealthy – thirty-five years earlier

D. Gordon's 'apothecarie and chymicall shop in New Aberdene' was selling both these perfumes for 6 shillings (30p, the cost of six fat geese) a grain (0.05g or 0.002oz).

To remedy sweating of the armpits, and other inconveniences proceeding thence

After the body hath been purged use a bath made with balm [balsam oil and resin], myrtle, lavender and other herbs of good scent in wine or water; therewith bathe the places affected, or else bathe them with wine and rosewater wherein you have boiled alum, myrrh, calamus aromaticus [sweet flag], lignum aloes, cloves.

If you bathe the armpits with any sort of alum dissolved in water it will condense the pores and hinder the sweat from straining through the skin. Or else you may often wash the armpits with white wine wherein nutmegs or mace have been boiled, or wherein three grains of musk have been dissolved; it hinders the transpiration of sweat and gives a pleasing odour to the body.

Monsieur Liebault, a French man, adviseth to keep this pomander under the armpits. Take styrax calamite, ladanum, benjamin, of each half a dram; cloves, mace, lignum aloes, lavender flowers, of each half a scruple; musk, one grain; with gum tragagant dissolved in rosewater and a little turpentine, make them up for use.
Artificial Embellishments, Thomas Jeamson, 1665

Lignum aloes is an aromatic wood from a tree native to Mexico, while styrax calamite is a sweet gum more often known as storax, and benjamin is a corruption of 'benjoin' or 'benzoin', another gum. The pomander is well known from sixteenth- and seventeenth-century images, but was originally the container for keeping a paste of mixed ingredients, then a perforated or fabric container from which the benefit of the paste could influence those in the vicinity, and then the mixture itself. In this case it could be a small bag of the mixture held in place under the arm by attachments to the clothes. It would have been a fairly pungent mix of aromas.

How to correct the ill scent of the arm-pits

The stink of the arm-holes makes some women very hateful; especially those that are fat and fleshy. To cure this, we may use such kinde of experiments. I dissolve allom in water, and I wash the feet and arm-pits with it, and let them dry; so in some days we shall correct the strong smell of those parts; but it will be done more effectually thus. Pound litharge of gold or silver, and boil it in vinegar; and if you wash those parts with it, you shall keep them a long time sweet; and it is a remedy, than there is none better.
Natural Magick, John Baptista Porta, 1669

Porta's directions are certainly not obscured by tact. He also gives recipes under the heading 'Some sports against women', such as 'To make a woman full of red pimples' and 'to make the face green', which no doubt his male readers found tremendously amusing.

An Anglo-Saxon cosmetic operation

Pound mastic very fine, add white of an egg and mix
as you do vermilion, cut with a knife, sew securely
with silk, then anoint with the salve outside and inside
before the silk rot. If it pulls together, arrange it with
the hand, anoint again immediately.
Leechdom II

This is the only known Anglo-Saxon description
of cosmetic surgery. The reference to vermilion, a
very expensive pigment, indicates that the intended
practitioner would have known the practices of
the scriptorium, where church manuscripts were
illuminated in brilliant colours. The condensed style
of writing also indicates that the text was directed at
people who would understand the basic principles —
the cut is to be made into the flesh. The silk, another
expensive import, would dissolve into the flesh, but
the mastic and egg mix appears to be applied as
prosthetic. The indication of aftercare shows a real
interest in the patient's well-being.

SOAPS AND CLEANSERS

'Never let the dust lie on the face after a long country drive or railway journey; it ruins the complexion', wrote 'A Professional Beauty' in *Beauty and How to Keep it* (1889).

Gentlemen's soaps

There are many soaps which are puffed off as 'the best article manufactured for shaving' – a 'beautiful preparation for softening the beard', etc.; but some of them are utterly worthless. All soaps are to be avoided which contain any considerable portion of alkalie; they make a light frothy lather that will not stand on the face. ... The soap which I have invariably found to be the best is Naples soap; it produces a beautifully mild creamy lather that will soften the beard, and will render shaving an agreeeable operation, and is best calculated to allay those smarting sensations ... on a tender skin. There is a great deal of white honey used in the manufacture of Naples soap ... there is nothing of a more mild and soothing nature.
The Gentleman's Companion to the Toilet, 'A London Hairdresser', 1844

To make the face fair

Take the flowers of rosemary and boil them in white wine,
then wash the face with it.
The Treasury of Commodious Conceits, 1584

This is a very long-standing recipe for a face wash, also known as Hungary water, from the antiquity of the recipe's use in that country.

Prepared sponges for the face

Steep in water some time the finest and thinnest sponges
you can pick out, wash them well, dry them, and then soak
them in brandy a whole day; then squeeze the brandy out
and dry them again; lastly dip them in orange flower water,
and let them remain therein eleven or twelve hours. When
squeezed and thoroughly dried they are now fit for use.
The Toilet of Flora, 1775

These sound quite delightful; if not still in use they should be.

How to cleanse the sweaty and sluttish complexion

The sluttish sordidness of some is often drowned in a
nasty deluge of sweat, out of a design perhaps to take
Cupid captive and birdlime his wings with such clammy

excrements; but if they have no other tempting bait than the greasy pomatum which their own ill-stuffed bodies supply them with, I am afraid (though being blind he cannot see them) he'll smell them a mile off and so keep his distance. They would do much better to break off this petty plot upon Cupid, and scour their bodies well with these abstersives.

Take bryony roots half a handful, lesser serpentary or friars coul, pellitory of the wall, of each three ounces; whole beans, rice, white vetch, French barley, of each two ounces and a half; flowers of camomile, melilot, of each one handful. Boil all these together in rain water, and receive the same up in the face. If you would have it for your whole body, double the quantities, pour them forth into a bath, set a stool in the bath, cast a sheet over you and so receive the vapour.

Artificial Embellishments, Thomas Jeamson, 1665

After Jeamson's tirade about sweaty bodies, his recipe for a steam bath does sound relaxing.

A remarkable face wash

Take a small piece of the gum benzoin and boil it in spirits of wine till it becomes a rich tincture. Fifteen drops of this, poured into a glass of water, will produce a mixture which will look like milk, and emits a most agreeable perfume.

This delightful wash seems to have the effect of calling the purple stream of the blood to the external fibres of the face, and gives the cheeks a beautiful rosy colour. If left on the face to dry, it will render the skin clear and brilliant. It

is also an excellent remedy for spots, freckles, pimples, and eruptions, if they have not been of long standing.
The Arts and Secrets of Beauty, Lola Montes, 1858

Lola Montes, mistress of the eccentric King Ludwig of Bavaria, dates this recipe to the time of Charles II. In her book on cosmetics she advises the reader to 'become her own manufacturer' in order to avoid the use of harmful concoctions at a time when increasing industrialisation often involved the use of adulterated ingredients.

To wash the face

There is no better thing to wash the face with, to keep it smooth and to scower it clean, than wash it every night with brandy wherein you have steeped a little flower of brimstone, and the next day wipe it only with a cloth.
The Compleat Servant-maid, Hannah Woolley, 1704

A wash for freckles

Take a quarter pound of bitter almonds, blanch them and beat them in a mortar, then put them in a pint of white wine; put to them two pennyworth of white poppy seeds and a large lemon; squeeze in the juice and then throw in the rind and let it stand a month close covered, then strain it out and put to it more a half pint of white wine; let it stand three days and then use it.
John Evelyn's papers, 1650s

AFTERWORD

Perfect beauty

To make a perfect beauty is required a smooth complexion, white and red, and each colour be truly placed, and those themselves imperceptibly the one in the other; which some ladies would express by the new French phrase demeslée. Full eyes, well made of a dark or black colour, graceful and casting a lustre. A nose well made, neither too big, nor too small. A little mouth, the upper lip resembling a heart in shape, and the under somewhat larger, but both of a vermilion colour, as well in winter as in summer; and on each side two small dimples easily to be discerned in their moving upwards, which look like a kind of constant smile. White teeth very clean, well ranged in order, of an equal bigness, neither short nor long, but very close set. A forked chin, not too long, and hanging double. A full sound or oval visage. The temples high raised. As for the colour of the hair opinions are various;

One the fair hair, another brown admires
A third a colour between both desires
But herein all concentre and do rest,
The colour of the loved object is the best
The Ladies Dictionary, 1694

LIST OF ILLUSTRATIONS